- A ☞ in the text denotes a highly recommended sight
- A complete A–Z of practical information starts on p.104
- Extensive mapping throughout: on cover flaps and in text

Berlitz Publishing Company, Inc.

Princeton   Mexico City   Dublin   Eschborn   Singapore

Text:	Donna Dailey
Editors:	Delphine Verroest, Peter Duncan
Photography:	Donna Dailey
Layout:	Media Content Marketing, Inc.
Cartography:	Visual Image

Thanks to Thomson Simply Greece, Auron Expeditions and Mr George Doukas of the Association of Corfu Travel Agents for their invaluable assistance in the preparation of this guide. Also thanks to Markella Callimassia.

Found an error we should know about? Our editor would be happy to hear from you, and a postcard would do. Although we make every effort to ensure the accuracy of all the information in this book, changes do occur.

ISBN 2-8315-6419-0
Revised 1998 – First Printing April 1998

Printed in Switzerland by Weber SA, Bienne
019/804 REV

CONTENTS

Corfu and the Corfiotes	7
A Brief History	13
Where to Go	25

Corfu Town 26
South from Corfu Town 44
The Northeast 50
The Northwest 58
The West Coast 66
Excursions 70

What to Do	79

Shopping 79
Entertainment 82
Sports 85
Children's Corfu 92

Eating Out	93
Index	101
Handy Travel Tips	104
Hotels and Restaurants	129

Fact Sheets

Historical Landmarks 18
Museum Highlights 38
Best Beaches — on cover
Festivals and Holy Days 90

Maps

Corfu Old Town 31

CORFU

CORFU AND THE CORFIOTES

Swathed in a blanket of deep green, its mountainous sky-line plunging into a crystal-clear, turquoise sea, Corfu is known as Greece's Emerald Island. Its many sunny beaches, spectacular landscape, and charming capital have enchanted visitors through the centuries. Fortunately, the beauty of this island has survived the mounting incursions of the modern world, with inviting, secluded places still scattered liberally along its fine coastline and throughout the hilly hinterland.

Corfu is the second-largest and most northerly of the Ionian islands—the others being Paxí, Levkas, Ithaca, Cephalonia, Zakinthos, and Kithera. Located only 74 km (46 miles) from Italy, Corfu has proudly styled itself Greece's western gateway and entry to the Adriatic. This enviable situation is one of the main reasons why, in atmosphere as well as geography, the island seems more Western than most other parts of Greece. Almost 500 years of Venetian, French, and British occupation have left their mark, most noticeably in the elegant architecture of Corfu Town. (Remarkably, the Turks—who conquered the rest of mainland Greece—failed to gain a foothold here.)

Corfu measures about 65 km (40 miles) in length and ranges in width from 4 to 30 km (2½ to 19 miles). Its shape resembles a scythe—in Greek *drépanon*, which was one of the ancient names for Corfu. According to geologists, the island is the exposed crown of a submerged mountain range that back in the recesses of time broke off from the mainland to its east.

This greenest of Greece's 1,425 genuine islands is arguably the prettiest as well. Flowering bushes, shrubs, and trees cloak most of its rolling landscape. In spring it is bursting with wildflowers, of which more than 100 varieties are to be found only here.

On the undulating hills and stone-hedged terraces of Corfu stand silvery groves of prized olive trees, their trunks knotted and gnarled, which provide excellent olive oil. The island is also graced with legions of orange and lemon trees giving off their glorious aroma, and plane trees, jacaranda, palms, wisteria, myrtle, oleander, and forests of tall, slim cypresses rising like sentries. Even the simplest homes are adorned with verdant grape arbours and enormous, beautiful clusters of roses or bougainvillaea.

There's a good reason for Corfu's remarkably luxuriant vegetation: more rain falls here—trapped by the nearby mainland mountains—than in any other part of Greece. For most of the year, however, this is very much an island in the sun.

Its 200-km (124-mile) coastline contains some of Europe's most beautiful—and cleanest—beaches. They vary

Mythical Beginnings

According to mythology, Poseidon, god of the sea, fell in love with the beautiful nymph Kórkyra, daughter of the river Assopós. He abducted her and took her to an island which adopted her name—today's Kérkyra (Corfu). In response Assopós endeavoured to pile up alluvium to fill the space between the island and the opposite shore. However, her efforts to reach her daughter were soon curtailed by Demeter, goddess of agriculture and sister of Poseidon. In order to help her brother—and protect the fertile island—Demeter entreated the almighty Zeus to stop the river's alluvial bridge.

Poseidon's union with Kórkyra produced Phaeax, the progenitor of the Phaeacians who, according to legend, were the first inhabitants of Corfu. Since ancient times the island has been identified with Schería, the "land of shadowy mountains" in Homer's *Odyssey*, where the civilized Phaeacians reigned.

from strips of pure sand to pebble or shingle, alone or mixed with sand, with a gradual or immediate drop to swimming depth, and rocks for diving. While swells for surfing may be found on the western shores, there exist plenty of calm bays suitable for children on the more protected east coast. As for the sea itself, in any one cove the range of clear blues seems to defy the colour spectrum.

Horse-drawn carriages have right-of-way in Corfu Town.

The sound of the sea slapping the shore, the twittering of a thousand birds, the braying of donkeys, the crowing of cocks—these are the musical motifs of Corfu. Adding to the medley, you'll almost always hear the strains of Greek traditional music. One of the Corfiotes' most beloved pastimes is singing: children and elders, in groups or on their own, sing happily and unselfconsciously.

One seldom-advertised feature of Corfu is the view that can be glimpsed of the towering mountains and sparsely inhabited coastline of **Albania**, which lies a mere 2 km (1½ miles) from Corfu's northeastern shore. Albania is now easily accessible by ferry and on a daytrip (see page 74).

About 108,000 people live on Corfu. Some of them do emigrate—attracted by life in the big city—but countless others have never left the island. Instead, the world comes to them, in sharply increasing numbers. Yet despite the seasonal influx of visitors, the inhabitants retain a fresh, open simplicity. The Corfiotes' legendary friendliness makes visitors feel very welcome.

The Corfiote pace of life is casual and unhurried. However, impatience does rear its head and is particularly in evidence at bus stops, shop counters, and bank tellers' windows, where only foreigners ever dream of queuing up docilely. Yet the islanders have their full measure of Greek *filótimo*, a quiet dignity and pride noticeable at all levels of society. A trip to the heart of the island will give you some insight into Corfiote village life. Time, in a number of places, seems to have stood still, and everyday life carries on pretty much as it has done for hundreds of years.

Home is where every Corfiote's heart really lies. Family life tends to be very close and affectionate, with an immense amount of attention lavished on small children. The Orthodox religion, with its elaborate ceremonies, is an intrinsic part of Corfiote life. Black-robed, bearded priests are a common sight all around the island.

Language is no problem for most visitors. A large number of Corfiotes speak English or Italian, and nearly all important signs are printed in both Greek and Latin alphabets.

The wonderful clear light and stunning landscape of the island have been a magnet for writers and artists throughout the centuries. Corfu is thought to have been the inspiration for settings in Homer's *Odyssey* and Shakespeare's "Tempest." In more recent times, the British painter Edward Lear depicted many views of Corfu's now famous sites, while the authors Lawrence and Gerald Durrell both lived here and were led to write entertaining books about island life. Many eminent foreigners, from the Rothschild family to the empress of Austria, have had villas built on the island.

Still the attraction remains: every year, from late March to early November, nearly a million visitors spend their vacations on Corfu. Approximately 60 percent of these tourists are British, followed by Germans, Italians, French, and a growing number of Eastern Europeans. Many are returning for the second, third, or perhaps even the twentieth time, such is the diverse nature of the island.

In recent years, Corfu has acquired an undeserved reputation as a "party" island, but non-stop nightlife occurs only in a small handful of resorts. In fact, Corfu has 44 resorts, with 44 different faces; most cater to families, and many are still relatively small and secluded. Though development has been rapid on parts of the island, it is less overbearing than in other holiday destinations, and the resorts are usually only

Corfiotes cherish family life and care deeply for their children.

really crowded in July and August. No matter where you are based, you can very easily get around and explore other parts of the island.

In 1994, Corfu hosted the European Union Summit. Millions of dollars were spent on constructing better roads, improving the island's airport, installing an entire new digital telephone system, and renovating many of the historic buildings in which the political events were hosted. The success of the Summit spurred the building of a new conference facility capable of accommodating 1,000 delegates, which opened in 1995.

Perhaps the most marvellous thing about Corfu, however, is that it has absorbed so much and yet changed so little. The majority of the island remains untouched by mass tourism. Peasant women supporting vast bundles of firewood ride along sidesaddle on their mules, barely glancing up at the jetliners overhead. Older village women still wear traditional headscarves and triple-layered dresses. Sleek sports cars roar off the ferries from Italy—and quickly slow to a gentle crawl behind 19th-century horse carriages. Gazing at the fishing nets hanging in the sun, one somehow feels that the beauty of this emerald island will endure.

Beautiful bougainvillea blossom everywhere.

A BRIEF HISTORY

Little is known of Corfu's first inhabitants. Prehistoric traces found at Gardiki in the southwest date back to the Palaeolithic era (70,000-40,000 B.C.), when the island was probably joined to the Greek mainland. Unlike on other Ionian islands, no traces of Mycenaean settlements have surfaced on Corfu, leading to speculation that it may have been held by the Phoenicians for the course of that period (1500-1150 B.C.).

Corfu's acknowledged history begins in 734 B.C., when the Corinthians established a colony called Corcyra, driving away Liburnian pirates. It was located south of today's Corfu Town in an area known as Paleópolis (old city). Archaeological digs (still in progress) have turned up evidence of temples near Kardáki Spring and Mon Repos (see page 42), but the ancient city was otherwise destroyed by barbarian raiders and its stone blocks were carried off to build the medieval town. The Gorgon

Ulysses and the Phaeacians

Shipwrecked during his 10-year voyage home from the Trojan War, Ulysses was washed ashore on the island of Schería. There he was found by Princess Nausicaa and her handmaidens when they came to wash clothes at a nearby stream. Nausicaa persuaded her father, the Phaeacian King Alcinous, to provide a boat to return him to his native Ithaca, but Alcinous' assistance angered Poseidon, who turned the ship to stone.

Three Corfu sites match the description in Homer's *Odyssey*: the Kanóni peninsula, Paleokastrítsa, and Afiónas. All have a double harbour approached by a narrow causeway, and an offshore rock that resembles a petrified ship—Mouse Island off Kanóni, Kolóvri off Paleokastrítsa, and Krávia island (meaning "ship") northwest of Cape Arílla. The beach where Ulysses was washed ashore is thought to be Ermónes, with its small stream.

pediment from the Temple of Artemis (sixth century B.C.), now in the Archaeological Museum (see page 38), is the single most important surviving artefact of classical Corcyra.

Prospering from trade with southern Italy, Corcyra soon set up her own colonies on the nearby mainland and grew into a strong maritime power. In 665 B.C., she defeated Corinth in what historian Thucydides noted to be the first naval battle in Greek history. Corcyra thus gained her independence.

Corfu's pact with Athens against Corinth and Sparta in 433 B.C. proved to be, according to Thucydides, the final straw that set off the Peloponnesian War and brought about the end of classical Greece. From then on, Corfu suffered attack, pillage, and often highly destructive occupation. Situated just 74 km (45 miles) from Italy and only 2 km (1½ miles) from Albania and the Greek mainland, Corfu's safe harbours, fertile soil, and strategic position between the Adriatic and Ionian seas made it a prize worth contesting by the myriad powers who fought for control of the region.

Roman Conquest

Before 200 B.C., a Roman fleet arrived and took over control of the island, making it the Roman Empire's earliest conquest across the Adriatic.

For the next five and a half centuries, Corfu prospered as a Roman naval base for forays into the mainland. En route to and from battles, or simply as tourists, Nero, Tiberius, Cato, Cicero, Caesar, Octavian, and Mark Antony (with Cleopatra) were among the Roman notables who visited Corfu.

Sometime before A.D. 200, St. Iáson (Jason) and St. Sosípatros brought Christianity to the island. The ruins of the sixth-century Paleópolis Church, located across from the entrance to Mon Repos, are among the few remnants left from Corfu's Roman period.

The Byzantine Years

When the Roman empire split in the fourth century A.D., the eastern half, Byzantium, took administrative control of Corfu, but could provide little security. Rampaging Vandals raided the island in 445. Even worse was to follow, in an invasion in 562 by a horde of Ostrogoths who, true to form, savagely destroyed Corfu's ancient capital and many monuments.

The Venetians' defensive moat at the Old Fort now harbors a collection of small boats.

After foiling an attempted takeover by Slavs in 933, the Corfiotes moved their capital 2 km (1½ miles) north and built their first fortress on the rocky bluff commanding the town's eastern sea approach; the Old Fort still stands. Elsewhere, islanders abandoned coastal settlements, and retreated inland to found the protective hill villages which remain a notable feature of the countryside.

Then appeared a formidable new enemy: several times between 1080 and 1185, Norman forces crossed the Ionian from Sicily to seize Corfu and nearby island outposts of the enfeebled Byzantine empire. Out of desperation Constantinople asked the Venetians for help. They responded and thereafter took an active interest in the destiny of this Adriatic gateway island.

When Doge Enrico Dandolo and the crusaders conquered Constantinople in 1204, the spoils claimed by Venice included western Greece, parts of the Peloponnese, and the Ionian islands; but Venice was unable to extend an immedi-

These olive groves are legacies of ancient ways.

ate reign over all its new holdings, and Corfu was left to a series of peaceable medieval occupying forces for some 200 years.

In 1214, Michaél Ángelos Comnenós, head of the Greek despotate of Epirus, took control; he built the fortresses of Angelokastro, high above Paleokastrítsa, and Gardíki on the west coast. In 1259 Corfu was presented to King Manfred, the Hohenstaufen king of Sicily, by Michael II as his daughter's dowry.

Eight years later, the new king of Sicily and Naples, Charles d'Anjou, became the overlord of Corfu; his family—the Angevins—ruled for over a century. During that time the traditional Eastern Orthodoxy of the island was almost extinguished by the newly official religion of Roman Catholicism.

Venetian Rule

When the Angevin dynasty ended, Corfu's fledgling assembly of 24 barons invited Venice to send in a protective military force. As always, marauding corsairs presented a danger. The Venetians landed on 20 May 1386, beginning an occupation that was to endure without interruption for over four centuries. The following year, Corfu officially became part of the Stato da Mar, the Venetian maritime empire.

Corfu prospered once again as a key port for galleys plying far-flung commercial routes. To strengthen the defences of its vital harbour, the Venetians turned Corfu Town's Byzantine fort into an impregnable bastion. It proved a wise move.

In 1463, having swept across mainland Greece, the Ottomans declared war on Venice. The Turks mounted assaults over succeeding years on the other Ionian islands. In 1537 it was Corfu's turn.

Intent on seizing the citadel, an Ottoman fleet led by the Barbary pirate Khair-el-Din (Barbarossa) landed cannons and troops north of the capital at Gouviá. The bitter attack on the fortress (renowned in Corfiote history) failed, but the rest of the island was looted and the vengeful Turks carried off 15,000 prisoners—nearly half the population. Most of them were bound into slavery.

Following the great siege, the Venetians dug a canal separating the Old Fort from the town. They also erected a "new fort"—which still answers to that name today—to guard the city's northwestern approach.

In 1571, Corfu sent 1,500 seamen to toil on Venetian galleys engaged in the famous naval battle of Lepanto, in the gulf of Patras, thus helping the Holy League of Christians to defeat the Moslem Turks. The last major confrontation of oared ships in history, this also marked the island's first naval triumph in many centuries.

Corfu's finest military hour was to come in 1716, once more against the Turks and once more at great cost. After losing both Athens and the Peloponnese to the Venetians, the Ottoman sultan successfully counter-attacked, retaking some Ionian islands, and sent 30,000 troops to quell Corfu.

Venice had hired foreign regiments under the German mercenary commander Johann Matthias von der Schulenburg to defend the island. For six bloody weeks the troops held out in

HISTORICAL LANDMARKS

734 B.C. Corinthians found colony of Corcyra.

665 B.C. Corcyra defeats Corinth and gains independence.

229 B.C.-A.D. 337 Romans take control of Corfu.

337-1081 The Roman Empire splits and Corfu falls under the administrative control of the Byzantine empire.

562 Ostrogoths destroy ancient capital city and monuments.

933 Corfiotes move capital farther north and build first fortress.

1080-1185 Normans from Sicily repeatedly invade Corfu.

1204 Fall of Constantinople; Venice gains control of Corfu.

1214-1259 Despots of Epirus take control of Corfu.

1266-1386 Angevin dynasty rules Corfu.

1386-1797 Long Venetian occupation establishes Corfu as a key port for commercial routes and important naval base.

1537 Corfiotes repel first Ottoman attack.

1571 Corfiotes beat Moslem Turks in naval battle at Lepanto.

1716 Second Ottoman attack on Corfu repelled.

1797-1814 French and Russians control Corfu.

1814-1863 Corfu becomes a British protectorate.

1827 Mainland Greece wins independence from Turks.

1864 Corfu and Ionia ceded to Greece; British withdraw.

1916 Corfu gives refuge to exiled Serbian government.

1941-43 Italians and Nazis occupy Corfu during W.W. II; Corfu Town very heavily damaged by bombardment.

1944 Corfu liberated by the Allies, after German evacuation.

1994 Corfu hosts European Union Summit.

Corfu Town. The Turks, with their overwhelmingly superior forces, ravaged the rest of the island and seemed about to capture the capital, when they suddenly called off their assault and fled, apparently frightened away by a ferocious thunder and hail storm and—the populace devoutly believes—the intervention of St. Spyrídon bearing a flaming torch. In any case, they did not return, and Corfu was the only part of Greece never to be subjugated by the Ottomans.

Throughout its long feudal occupation, Venice kept Corfu firmly in tow, a colony valued as an important naval base, trading depot, customs-collection station, and supply centre. A civil-military governor and senior bureaucrats sent from Venice ran the island. A Golden Book listing the Corfiote nobility, like Venice's *Libro d'Oro*, contained 277 families at the end of the Venetian rule.

Ordinary islanders, however, were heavily taxed and denied public education. Nothing was done to restore the Greek Orthodox religion to its traditional dominance among the doggedly faithful people. Italian replaced Greek as the official language, even though the peasantry couldn't understand it and had no way of learning it. Many laboured as serfs in the Venetian aristocrats' villas which still dot the countryside.

More happily, Venice was reponsible for nearly all the olive trees that grace Corfu's landscape: anxious to ensure a constant supply of oil, the republic at one stage decreed a cash bonus for every 100 trees planted. This new olive production permanently changed the island's economy for the better. An even more visible legacy, however, is Corfu's old city: with its narrow streets and tall buildings, it's the most Venetian town in Greece.

Napoleon's Dream Island

In 1797, the republic of the doges fell to Napoleon, thus ending 411 years of Venetian occupation. For reasons which remain obscure, Napoleon was rather obsessed with the island. "The greatest misfortune which could befall me is the loss of Corfu," he wrote to his foreign minister, Talleyrand. So, immediately after capturing Venice, Napoleon sent a force to occupy Corfu and the other Ionian islands, which soon passed legally to France.

These French occupiers replaced Venice's autocratic rule with new democratic representation, burned Corfu Town's Golden Book, introduced public education, and made Greek the official language. Nevertheless, they still managed to antagonize the island's inhabitants by continuing to suppress the Orthodox Church. Within two years, the French were driven out of the island by a joint Russo-Turkish force that reinstated Greek Orthodoxy as the official religion

The Old-Fort clock tower stands tall in the city as a reminder of a bygone Venetian time.

In 1807, the Bonapartists regained Corfu from the Russians by the Treaty of Tilsit. Napoleon—never actually able to visit what he called "the key to the Adriatic"—garrisoned the citadels with 50,000 men along with 500 new cannon, making the island one of the most powerful fortified points in the eastern Mediterranean.

The French then established the first Ionian Academy for the promotion of arts and sciences, imported Greece's first printing presses, drew a street plan for Corfu Town, built a miniature Rue de Rivoli (the Listón), and began the growing of potatoes and tomatoes, now mainstays of Corfiote cooking.

During this time, the British carried on an ineffectual but irritating blockade of the island. They seized four other Ionian islands from the French, but had no hope of taking Corfu.

The British Move In

Napoleon's luck ran out. After his ill-judged attack on Russia and his subsequent abdication, the British took Corfu. A year later, in 1815, the Treaty of Vienna turned the seven Ionian Islands into one independent state under British protection. Corfu then became the capital, and Sir Thomas Maitland, the Lord High Commissioner.

The British occupation of Corfu lasted for half a century. While controversial, this protectorate brought certain benefits. Under Maitland, a road network was built. His successor had the road to Paleokastrítsa constructed, and brought a permanent water-supply system to Corfu Town. While a number of changes were pure personal caprice on the part of the ten British High Commissioners, they also brought hospitals, model prisons, a decent judiciary, and religious freedom ensuring the primacy of the Orthodox Church. The slightly eccentric Lord Guilford, a philhellene who went about in classical Greek dress, established Greece's first university, the Ionian Academy, here in 1824. He bequeathed it his library of 25,000 books, and helped to make Corfu the country's chief literary and intellectual centre of its day.

The constitution set in place by Maitland (1817) was another matter. Though maintaining a façade of parliamentary government with a Corfiote senate and assembly, the High Commissioner retained all power. Serious unrest first occurred in the 1820s. Mainland Greece was engaged in the war of independence against Turkey, but Maitland stopped the Corfiotes from giving assistance to their Greek compatriots. This engendered widespread bitterness among the islanders.

As sentiment for union with the mainland rose after Greece gained independence in 1827, the British introduced token constitutional reforms, freeing the press and liberalizing election procedures. However, the High Commissioner's power remained intact. Nationalistic agitation for union—*énosis*—

The First European

Corfu's most famous son is Ioánnis Kapodístrias. Born of a noble family, he became Greece's first president in 1827. He is hailed as the first statesman to envisage a unified Europe.

With the collapse of the Venetian Empire in 1797, he was instrumental in the creation of the Federation of Ionian Islands. He then served as a diplomat in the Russian court of Tsar Alexander. On a mission to Switzerland in 1813, he orchestrated the Swiss Federation, which has remained in place to this day. Two years later, at the Congress of Vienna, he again protected Swiss interests against other European powers.

In the ensuing years he began to develop ideas of a unified Europe in which no one member should become too powerful, and in which the powers would collectively regulate the whole. In this, he was a man ahead of his time. Fittingly, in 1994, his home island hosted the very Union of which he had dreamed.

continued to grow until even the most stubborn colonialist saw the writing on the wall.

Greek at Last

When the pro-British Prince William of Denmark became King George I at Athens in 1863, Corfu and the other six Ionian islands were ceded to Greece as a gesture of goodwill to the new monarch. An agreement drawn up by the big powers declared the islands "perpetually neutral," and before hauling down the Union Jack, the British blew up the impressive fortifications they had added to Corfu Town. When they sailed off, the island's assembly made known its gratitude to Queen

A Corfu woman proudly shows off her traditional and colourful costume.

Victoria for this unprecedented voluntary withdrawal by a great power from an overseas possession.

Behind them the British left a number of stately buildings and monuments. Cricket, ginger beer, and Christmas chutney are other British legacies that remain favourites today.

Peace settled on the island in its early years as a province of Greece. Aristocratic tourists converged here; Empress Elisabeth of Austria liked it so much that she commissioned an elaborate palace south of Corfu Town (see page 26).

Though officially a neutral country during World War I, Corfu served as an Allied military and naval base, recalling the role the island had played in previous centuries. In 1916 Corfu gave refuge to the exiled government of Serbia and its troops after they were driven from the mainland. Thousands died from wounds and disease and now lie in the Serbian cemetery on Vídos Island. The next year, the Serbs signed the Declaration of Corfu, laying the foundations of the Yugoslavia that fell apart in the 1990s.

In 1923, Mussolini gave an order for his fleet to bombard the island in reprisal for the alleged assassination of one of his generals on the Albanian-Greek border. Italian forces occupied Corfu briefly until they were obliged to withdraw under diplomatic pressure (primarily from Great Britain).

The Italians returned as occupiers in World War II. Mussolini issued new currency and renamed streets, signalling his intention to annex the Ionian islands. However, Italy subsequently capitulated in 1943.

When the Germans tried to succeed their defeated allies, the Italian troops resisted on both Corfu and its sister island of Paxí. In the ensuing battle, nearly one-quarter of Corfu Town was destroyed, including the Ionian parliament house, the academy, and the municipal theatre. After a year of occupation, German forces evacuated from Corfu in October 1944. The British moved in behind them, and peace descended once more.

Corfu was largely unaffected by the Greek civil war between communist and royalist partisans which raged on the mainland between 1947 and 1949. Since then, tourism and agriculture—the two economic mainstays of the island— have brought unprecedented prosperity to much of Corfu.

Corfu's shining hour came in 1994 when it hosted the European Union Summit, which marked the end of the Greek presidency of the E.U. This national honour confirmed the island's status as one of the most forward-looking and development-prone areas in Greece.

WHERE TO GO

V isitors generally tend to stay at resorts outside Corfu Town, coming in to shop or visit the old churches, fortresses, and museums. Allow plenty of time to enjoy the island's atmospheric capital, with its many handsome public buildings and lovely sea views along Garítsa Bay. Feel free to wander leisurely underneath the arcades and along the flagstone streets of the old quarter, admiring the tall, shuttered houses with graceful wrought-iron balconies. Don't be surprised if you frequently find yourself drawn back to this appealing town, where simply sitting with a cool drink and a pretty view leaves a profound sense of well-being.

A Corfu woman treks along a country road on the outskirts of the town.

No matter where you stay, try to spend at least one day exploring other parts of Corfu. Public buses run from Corfu Town to the main towns and resorts, though you may find the schedules confining. Your best bet is to hire a car so that you can tour at your leisure and reach the off-the-beaten-track villages, roads, and beaches which offer some of Corfu's most rewarding experiences.

Glimpsed from street level, the belfry of St. Spyridon towers high above Corfu Town.

CORFU TOWN

The old city of Corfu is a beguiling town, with a relaxed, old-world elegance which rivals other Mediterranean cities many times its size. Its predominately Venetian architecture is harmoniously flavoured with French and English Georgian building styles, reflecting the influence of several centuries of foreign occupation. A cosmopolitan nature still prevails, especially at night-time, when both Corfiotes and visitors stroll along the Listón and rendezvous at the many outdoor cafés and restaurants.

Corfu Town grew up on the eastern peninsula around the Old Fort, which was erected for protection from barbarian raiders in the tenth century. The two peaks of the promontory on which it stands—strikingly apparent from offshore—were the inspiration for the name, Koryphó (*koryfí* means "summit" in Greek). A coastal road lined with graceful lamp-posts follows the medieval sea walls and offers stunning views of the fortress and harbour.

Around the Esplanade

The focal point of Corfu Town is the **Esplanade** *(Spianáda)*. Families promenade, marching bands parade, and festive occasions are frequently celebrated on this broad, green expanse separating the Old Fort from the rest of town. The area was razed in Venetian times to give a clear field of fire against enemy assault; it was also used for fairs and jousting tournaments. The French later planted the palms, eucalyptus trees, and flower gardens.

The **Ionian Monument** on the southern half of the Esplanade celebrates the island's union with Greece in 1864 and is surrounded by marble reliefs displaying the symbols of the seven Ionian islands. Nearby is the Victorian bandstand where Sunday concerts are held in summer, and, farther along, the Maitland Rotunda, dedicated to the first British High Commissioner. At the far end is the statue of Greece's first president (1827-31), Corfu's greatest son, Ioánnis Kapodístrias.

The Esplanade's most famous landmark is its **cricket pitch**, dominating the northern half. Corfu inherited this sport during the British rule, and enthusiastic local teams keep the tradition alive with matches during the season. You're likely to see visiting British teams at the wicket, playing against local opponents, to the cheers and groans of fans sipping drinks under the trees.

Across the north side of the Esplanade stands the imposing **Palace of St. Michael and St. George**, erected between 1818 and 1823 as the residence for the British High Commissioners. It also housed the Ionian senate and the Order of St. Michael and St. George, which honoured British civil

The Esplanade provides an usually atmospheric setting for an afternoon cricket match.

servants of distinction in Malta and the Ionian islands. The limestone structure, with its Neo-classical façade of 32 Doric columns linking triumphal arches, was designed by the architect Sir George Whitmore. When the British left, Greek royalty used it as a summer residence. The European Union Summit talks were held here in 1994.

A bronze, toga-clad figure stands above a lily pond in front of the palace. It's that of Sir Frederick Adam, Britain's second High Commissioner, sculpted by Corfiote artist Pávlos Prosaléntis. The pool and its little water spouts are there to remind people that Adam was the first to ensure Corfu Town a reliable water supply, with an aqueduct system still in use today.

The state rooms, open to the public, now house the remarkable **Museum of Asiatic Art**. This collection of over 10,000

Asian artefacts was amassed by Grigórios Mános, a former Greek diplomat. Other donors have made it one of the most comprehensive collections of its kind in the world. Ancient pieces include Chinese funerary statuary and bowls, some almost 3,000 years old, as well as pottery and ceramics from the course of half a dozen Chinese dynasties—Chou ritual bronzes, Ming Buddhas, and decorative T'sing dishware. Among other displays from Japan, Thailand, Nepal, Tibet, Korea, and India are intricate screens, ancient Khmer stone heads, armour, silks, and ivory. You'll also find an interesting collection of post-Byzantine Christian art containing a number of icons, some evocative frescoes, and stone engravings.

The elegant arcades of the **Listón** border the west side of the Esplanade. Inspired by the Rue de Rivoli in Paris, it was built by the French in 1807. Its name comes from the "list" of noble families who were the only ones permitted to walk here (see page 19). Today everyone gathers at the many cafés and bars under the arches, or beneath the acacia trees along the

---

That's Cricket

The cricket pitch on Spianáda Square is one of the most striking sportsgrounds in the world. Kim Hughes, the Australian captain during the early 1980s, once hit a mighty six right over the gardens and into the moat of the Old Fort here.

The mixed cultural heritage of the island can be heard in the cricketing language. "Play" is the Corfiote name for cricket, but, perhaps on account of the long association with the Venetians, more than one term used during play has been lifted from Italian. When a "long hop" turns into "primo salto" and cricket stumps are "xyla" (wood in Greek), the English may feel at a loss in their own game. Still, when England ex-captain David Gower was asked where he had enjoyed playing the most, his immediate reply was, "It has to be Corfu."

green. During the evening, this pedestrian-only street is transformed into a promenade of Corfiotes and visitors alike, from dapper elderly men to smartly dressed families.

Dousmáni Street cuts across the Esplanade to the Old Fort. Here you'll find an information kiosk, as well as a string of colourful horse-cabs (*carrozza*) for hire. These handsome 19th-century buggies will take you on a ride around Corfu Town. Be sure to agree on the fare before you set out.

A statue of Count Schulenburg, the German mercenary who led the Corfiote defence against the Turkish attack of 1716 (see page 17), stands outside the entrance to the **Old Fort**. A defensive moat, the Contrafossa, now lined with small boats, separates the Old Fort from the rest of town. This was one of the many fortifications added by the Venetians to the older Byzantine citadel on the eastern peak. In those days the bridge could be lifted, cutting off all access to the fort.

The Venetian seat of government here was destroyed by the British, who built barracks and a military hospital (used by the Greek army until 1979). Restoration has been going on ever since. Extensive improvements were made to the fort for the European Summit in 1994, and the first thing that you are likely to notice as you pass through the huge vaulted gateway is the brick building which now houses a high-tech telecommunications centre.

Beyond, a path to your right leads to the garrison church of St. George, built by the British in 1840 as an Anglican chapel and restored after damage during World War II. Nowadays this pseudo-Doric temple is used as an exhibition hall for museum displays.

A stone path leads past a Venetian clocktower, up to the lighthouse on the higher peak. The steep climb is worth it for the spectacular panorama of Corfu Town, the harbour, and Mount Pantokrátor to the north.

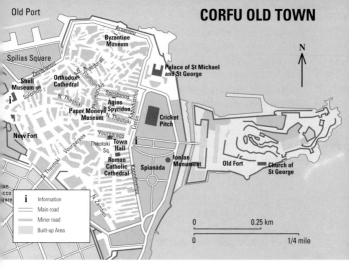

The Old Town

By all means get lost in the Old Town, or Campiello—the endlessly fascinating maze of narrow streets, steep stairways, and arched alleys pinched between the Old Fort and the Old Port. As you wander along the flagstoned streets, peeking into people's open houses and examining shop wares, you may soon feel that this traffic-free, tall-walled quarter is like a miniature Venice—minus all the canals. In Venetian times the area between the old and new forts was surrounded by city walls (torn down during the 19th century) for defensive reasons. As Corfiotes weren't permitted to live outside the walls, the only direction in which they could expand their living quarters was upwards, hence the unusually high buildings.

Make sure you go beyond the few busy streets lined with shops that branch off from the Esplanade. Much of the Old

Town's appeal is strictly residential, with laundry strung across its alleyways, costumed old women on stools weaving or keeping an eye on babies, and cats snoozing in tiny sun-splashed squares.

From the northern end of the Listón, continue your walk along Kapodistríou Street. Just past the palace is one of the town's loveliest buildings, the **Corfu Reading Society**, with its exterior staircase leading up to a small loggia. It is the oldest cultural institution in modern Greece, and contains the history of the Ionian Islands in an archival collection of photographs, books, manuscripts, and other documents.

At the top of the street, a marvellous little corniche road—Arséniou Street—girdles the Old Town along the sea wall. The green island visible offshore is **Vídos**, the base for Ottoman assaults in 1537 and 1716. Its fortications were destroyed when the British left the island in 1864, and subsequently it became a prison. Today its shady paths harbour a bird sanctuary, which can be visited from the Old Port.

Icons Itinerant

From the fall of Constantinople to the Ottomans (1453) until 1669, Crete under Venetian occupation proved to be Greece's most important artistic centre. A school of art flourished in icon painting, attracting commissions from monasteries and noblemen abroad.

Lying at the crossroads between east and west, Corfu became an important stepping stone for Cretan painters seeking economic and cultural support en route to Venice. Emmanuel Tzanés is credited with introducing the Cretan style of church painting to the island in the 17th century, and his works can be seen on display in the Byzantine Museum and several churches in Corfu Town. Many other artists found refuge on the island after Crete fell to the Ottomans in 1669. Thus a vital force in Byzantine traditional art was kept alive on Corfu.

A flight of steps from Arséniou leads to the recently re-opened **Byzantine Museum**, which is housed in the 15th-century basilica of Antivouniótissa (church of the Holy Virgin). The single-aisle, timber-roofed church is one of the oldest and richest on the island, constructed in the traditional Corfiote manner with a vestibule around three sides. In the museum there is an impressive array of icons ranging from the 13th to the 17th centuries.

Lighting a prayer candle: Religion is a way of life.

Around the corner, a magnificent profile of the New Fort comes into view. Below you lies the Old Port, from where you can catch ferries for Paxí and Igoumenítsa. Fronting the ferry port is George II Square (Plateía Georgíou B), sometimes known as Spiliás Square after the nearby Spiliá Gate, one of four gates through the medieval city walls. There is a local bus stop here.

Also known as the Fort of San Marco, the **New Fortress** was built by the Venetians in 1576, shortly after the second of two major Turkish sieges. You can see their emblem, the winged lion of St. Mark, in stone relief above the massive gates. The French, and later the British, completed the fortifications. It's here, in the dry moat on the western side, that the town's fruit and vegetable market is now held. A series of secret tunnels is said to connect the new and old fortresses. You can explore a few of the tunnels and underground dungeons inside the fortress, and also take a look round the exhi-

A silver coffin and relics of St. Spiridon displayed at church.

bitions that are held here. From the top of the fort, you'll be rewarded with fine views of Corfu Town and the far coast.

From New Fortress Square near the entrance, Solomoú Street leads to the delightful **Shell Museum**. This amazing show of seashells, corals, fossils, starfish, and sponges was gathered from throughout the world by Corfiote Napoléon Sagiás, and is one of the best private shell collections in Europe. The many specimens on display range from very large melo amphora shells to tiny delicate cowries, shark's jaws, spiny crustacean skeletons, and stuffed puffer fish. In addition, there's a curious assortment of pickled creatures floating in ominous jars of formaldehyde.

At the end of the street, veer right and go along N. Theotóki Street (note the first initial—there are several streets named after members of this long-established, illustrious Corfiote family). Beyond the Hotel Crete, adorned with a row of curious carved heads, is **Ionikí Square**, named after the Ionian Bank building which commands the western side. The island's oldest bank (opened in 1839), the Ioanian has the **Paper Money Museum** on its first floor, with an extensive display ranging from early Ionian banknotes to world currency. An impressive exhibit details all the stages in designing, printing, and releasing notes for circulation.

In the centre of the square there stands a statue of Corfiote politician Geórgios Theotókis (1843-1916). Across from the bank stands the **Faneroméni** church, also called Our Lady of the Strangers (Panagía Ton Xénon) because it was lived in by refugees from the mainland during the time of the Turkish occupation there. Erected in 1689, it is lavishly decorated with gilded wood, a beautifully painted ceiling, and icons by the Cretan painters (see page 32). The rather lighter and simpler **St. John the Baptist** (Ágios Ioánnis o Pródromos) on the

---

St. Spyrídon

Corfiotes pray to him, swear by him, name their sons after him, and honour him with truly remarkable passion. He is the island's beloved patron saint, yet he wasn't even born here.

Spyrídon was a village shepherd on the distant island of Cyprus who became a monk, and later a bishop, noted for his devoutness and ability to effect minor miracles. After his death in a.d. 350, a sweet odour wafted from his grave; his body was exhumed and found to be perfectly preserved. The saint's remains were taken to Constantinople, but were smuggled out (with those of St. Theodóra Augusta) before the Turkish occupation in 1453. Unceremoniously wrapped in a sack of straw strapped to a mule, the remains arrived in Corfu in 1456, and in time Spyrídon became the object of enthusiastic veneration.

His casket is paraded through Corfu Town in colourful processions on Orthodox Palm Sunday, Easter Saturday, 11 August, and the first Sunday in November to honour his miracles.

St. Spyrídon reputedly saved the island four times: twice from the plague, once from famine, and once (in 1716) from the Turks. Small wonder that most Corfu men are named Spíros.

south side of the square, built in 1520, was formerly Corfu's cathedral and contains important Cretan paintings.

The red-domed bell-tower of **Ágios Spyrídon**, the tallest on the island, rises north of the square. It was built in 1590 to house the mummified body of Corfu's beloved saint, who lies in an ornate silver coffin in a chapel to the right of the altar. On special feast days the casket is opened, and the saint is paraded upright through town; his shrunken face can be seen through a glass panel and his slippered feet are exposed for the faithful to kiss. With all the rich Venetian oil lamps swinging above the casket, the chandeliers, and the candelabra, this rather small, dimly lit church is thought to have the greatest weight of silver of any Greek church outside the island of Tínos. Paintings on the ceiling depict the saint's miracles.

Outside the church, turn left into Ágios Spirídonos Street and, at the end, turn right into Filarmonikis, then left again into Filellínon, a narrow passageway lined with shops. The maze-like streets that make up the **Campiello**, Greece's largest living "medieval" town, lie to your right. As you emerge from Filellínon, turn right into Ágios Theódoros. Look for a short flight of steps on the left, which lead to Kremastí Square and the lovely **Venetian well**, inscribed in 1699. One of the island's best restaurants opens here in the evenings (see page 135).

By retracing the route along Ágios Theódoros you'll reach Corfu's **Orthodox cathedral**, built in 1577 and dedicated to St. Theodóra, the island's second saint. Her headless body, which was spirited out of Constantinople with Spyrídon's, lies in a silver reliquary to the right of the altar screen. She is greatly adored by the population even though she performs no miracles. There's a serene, slightly Eastern beauty to this small church. Broad flights of steps in front of the cathedral lead down to the harbour, and Greek voyagers often momentarily pause here to light a candle before or after a crossing.

Back at the Esplanade, stroll down the length of **Kapodis-tríou Street**, which runs from behind the Listón to the southern end of the green. It is lined with handsome homes, most of which were built by the aristocracy. At the end is the pink façade of the old Ionian Academy, which once housed Lord Guilford's library (see page 21). Like much of the surrounding area, it was destroyed in the heavy bombing of 1943.

Several picturesque streets lead into town. Moustoxídou Street used to be an important thoroughfare, and also the setting for jousting displays during Carnival, with the judges seated on the balcony above the ornate portico of the Ricchi mansion.

Turn right at Gilfórdou Street, which leads into **Plateía N. Theotóki**, once the main square of the old town. Ahead of you is the **Town Hall**, one of Corfu's most decorative buildings. Built by the Venetians in 1663 out of white marble from the eastern slopes of Mount Pantokrátor, its original single-storey loggia served as a meeting place for the

The ornate town hall lies like an achor at the bottom of the lovely N. Theotóki Square.

MUSEUM HIGHLIGHTS

Hours and prices are correct at the time of printing, but should be checked with the tourist office on arrival. All museums have reduced admission for students, and are free to students of EU countries.

Archaeological Museum. 5 Vraíla Street; tel. 30680. Highlights include a gigantic Gorgon pediment from the Temple of Artemis (sixth century b.c.) and an archaic lion from the Tomb of Menecrates. 800drs. Open Tues-Sun 8.45am-3pm. (See page 39)

Art Gallery. Castelino at Káto Korakiána, near the resort of Dassiá; tel. 93333. This department of the Greek National Art Gallery in Athens offers changing exhibitions. Open summer 10am-1pm and 6-9pm, winter 10am-1pm; closed Mon. (See page 52)

Byzantine Museum. Off Arséniou Street; tel. 38313. Beautiful icons and paintings from the 16th to 18th centuries, housed in the late-15th-century basilica of Antivouniótissa. 800drs. Open Tues–Sun 9am–3pm. (See page 33)

Museum of Asiatic Art. Palace of St. Michael and St. George, Esplanade; tel. 30443. A remarkable collection from China, Japan, and other Far Eastern cultures amassed by a former Greek diplomat. 400drs. Open daily 8:45am-3pm; closed Mon. (See page 28)

Paper Money Museum. Ionian Bank of Corfu, 1st floor, St. Spyrídon Square; tel. 41552. An extensive display of Greek banknotes from 1820 to the present day, foreign notes from around the world, and an impressive exhibit on how a banknote is designed and created. Free. Open Mon-Fri 9am-1pm. (See page 34)

Shell Museum. 7-9 Solomoú Street; tel. 42900. An amazing collection of shells, corals, sponges, and other sea creatures from several continents. 500drs. Open daily 10am-7pm. (See page 34)

Sinarádes History and Folklore Museum. 2 Spage Nikokávoura Street, Sinarádes village; tel. 38193. This village home with its original furnishings offers an authentic look at Corfiote life as it used to be in the last century. 200drs. Open daily 9:30am-2:30pm; closed Mon. (See page 68) nobility. It was converted into a theatre in 1720 and later a second storey was added. It became the Town Hall in 1903. The façade is adorned with carved masks and medallions. On the eastern wall there is a bust of Francesco Morosini, a Venetian commander who defeated the Turks at Athens in 1687 and was in charge when a stray shell hit the Parthenon.

On the eastern side of the square is the **Roman Catholic cathedral**. It was very badly damaged during World War II, and fragments of the former structure are kept in the side chapels. Its simple, pale-peach interior makes a light, airy and peaceful retreat.

A magnificent set of steps and flower-bedecked terraces ascends above the square. The stately building at the top was originally the Catholic Archbishop's palace; subsequently it was converted into the Law Courts; now it is home to the Bank of Greece.

Since Venetian times, there have been silversmiths practising their trade along Voulgáreos Street, which runs behind the Town Hall. It ends at a tiny roundabout, near where the western gate of the old town walls, the Porto Reale, used to stand. The striking Venetian bell tower belongs to a 16th-century Catholic church. From here, G. Theotóki Street carries on through the present-day town towards Plateía G. Theotóki, better known as San Rocco Square, a busy, traffic-laden commercial centre. This is the point from which local buses arrive and depart.

The Archaeological Museum

Corfu's archaeological museum lies close to the centre of town, just a few minutes' walk south of the Esplanade. For a pleasant stroll to the museum, follow the coastal road along Garítsa Bay, turning right after the Corfu Palace hotel.

This pleasantly modern and airy museum houses two of the finest works of antiquity ever found. The featured attraction is the **Gorgon pediment**, originating from a 6th-century B.C. Temple of Artemis at ancient Corcyra (see page 13). It derives its name from the ferocious, sculpted Medusa (one of three snake-haired gorgons), shown here with wings at her back and shoes, and serpents at her waist. She is flanked by Pegasus, the winged horse, and the hero Chrysáor, Medusa's own offspring, born from her dying blood. Beside her stand two alert lion-panthers waiting to obey the first command of this monster who, according to the myth, instantly turned all who gazed upon her face to stone. The pediment was discovered in 1912 at Paleópolis and has undergone expert restorations. It is Greece's oldest existing monumental sculpture.

Not so colossal but every bit as fearsome is the **archaic lion** that lies atop a pedestal in the adjoining room. This remarkable sculpture, dating from the same period as the Gorgon pediment, was found near the Tomb of Menecrates in 1843 and is thought to have graced the grave of a warrior during Corfu's struggle for independence from Corinth. The lion was chiselled by an unknown Corinthian artist and is considered one of the most beautiful ancient animal sculptures.

The ancient church of St. Jason and Sosipatros.

Among the museum's other treasures, which include pottery, coins, bronze statuettes, figurines, and Neolithic artefacts, look out for the series of small statues depicting the goddess Artemis in her different guises as huntress, protector, and guardian of the hearth. They are thought to have been produced for local worshippers—in what may have been Corfu's first souvenir shop.

On the Outskirts

A few minutes' walk from the middle of the town, the serenely beautiful **British Cemetery** retains special significance for a large number of British and Commonwealth visitors. Between the tall cypress trees and meticulously kept flowers and shrubbery lie graves that date back to the start of Britain's protectorate, as well as those of British servicemen from the two World Wars. The circular wall south of the cemetery encloses the penitentiary. Built by the British, it was once the most modern penal institute in Europe, with individual cells for inmates. It is in use today.

The **Tomb of Menecrates** lies south of Corfu Town, one block inland from the monument to Sir Howard Douglas, another High Commissioner, at the intersection of the coastal road and Alexandras Avenue. This circular stone crypt with its conical roof was a tribute to a foreigner who served on the mainland in Corcyra's interests, and dates from about 600 B.C. It lies in a garden next to the traffic-police station.

Keep going south along the bay past Garítsa, which was a separate village in the British period and a popular spot for a Victorian seaside promenade. At the suburb of Anemómylos, veer inland to the Byzantine **Church of Ágii Iáson and Sosípatros** (Saints Jason and Sosípatros). Built out of limestone, brick, and tile, this is one of only two surviving Byzantine churches on the island. It dates back to the 12th century, though earlier versions stood here during Corfu's Byzantine epoch (337-1204). The black marble columns separating the vestibule and a number of the large blocks used for the walls are thought to be from Classical buildings.

The whitewashed interior is well lit and refreshing. At the entrance, place of honour goes to two very beautiful 16th-century icons by Cretan painter Emmanuel Tzanés, portraying Iáson of Tarsus and Sosípatros of Ikónion, the militant saints credited with bringing Christianity to the island in the second century. The church is generally open throughout the day.

Farther along the road to Kanóni stands the entrance to the villa and gardens of **Mon Repos**. Built in 1831 by the High Commissioner Frederick Adam as a summer residency, and subsequently dubbed "Sir Frederick's folly," it later became the property of the Greek royal family. Prince Philip, the duke of Edinburgh, was born here in 1921. The villa has been spendidly restored and may be visited by appointment only; check with the guard for information. You can also enjoy the peaceful splendour of the extensive gardens; paths wind along the wooded promontory, past an old chapel with vine-covered arbours up to a scenic view of the shore below. You can swim at the beach for a small charge.

The Ancient City

Opposite the Mon Repos gate lie the commanding ruins of **Agía Kérkyra**, or Paleópolis Church. The fifth-century basilica is the oldest church on the island, constructed from remnants of far older pagan temples that once stood on the site. It was destroyed by invaders and rebuilt several times in the ensuing centuries, and brought to its present state only by the bombing of World War II.

The original eighth-century B.C. Corinthian city sprawled over much of this area, now called **Paleópolis**, and you'll see archaeological digs in progress. The side opposite the basilica leads to the hamlet of Análypsis, thought to be the acropolis of the ancient city of Corcyra. From the church at the top of the hill there is a superb view of the Mon Repos grounds. A new archaeological park to appear at Paleópolis will present the ruins of four temples, ancient dockyards, and artefacts from the excavations.

Close by the roundabout at Análypsis, a steep path leads down to the **Kardáki Spring**. The water, flowing cool in the summer and warm in the winter from the mouth of a lion, is reputed never to dry up. Legend has it that anyone who drinks from the spring is destined to return to Corfu.

Back up the path, inside the Mon Repos estate, is a small Doric temple that dates from around 500 B.C., probably dedicated to Poseidon. Along the road towards Kanóni, down a side road signposted "Stratia," are the ruins of the **Temple of Artemis**—where the Gorgon in the Archaeological Museum (see page 39) was excavated. Next door is the Convent of Ágios Theódoros. Farther along the road stands one of the sections of the wall of ancient Corcyra, dating from the fifth century B.C.

The Venerable Olive

Almost everyone on Corfu owns a few olive trees. They proliferated greatly during Venetian times, when peasants were paid for each tree they planted, so much so that by the 17th century a family's wealth was determined by the number of trees it owned. Today there are 3 1/2 million on the island!

According to legend, St. Spyrídon appeared in an olive grove and proclaimed that cutting or beating the trees was cruel. Corfiotes neither prune the branches nor pick the fruit, but let the olives fall to the ground of their own accord, where huge nets are spread to catch them. Trees bear fruit only every other year, and may take 12 years to yield a first crop.

SOUTH FROM CORFU TOWN

Two of Corfu's most visited sights—Mouse Island and the Achílleion Palace—lie just a few kilometres south of Corfu Town. You can reach them by public buses, or join one of the organized excursions available (see page 114 and page 125).

signs:
ΑΦΙΞΗ- Arrival
ΑΝΑΧΩΡΗΣΗ-
Departure

Kanóni

Generations of earlier visitors once knew **Kanóni** as a tranquil, green peninsula, a short, pleasant walk or carriage ride south of the capital. Popular with Corfiotes, it also used to attract large groups of British residents, who came to admire the most famous view on the island, that of the two islets resting peacefully in the Chalikiópoulos lagoon.

Times have changed, however. New hotels and blocks of flats have unfortunately disfigured the landscape—though the motives for building here are hard to ascertain, as most of the windows have a view only of the shallow and murky lagoon and an adjacent airport runway, with sound effects.

Nevertheless, the delightful, picture-postcard view of the islets and the pleasant coastal scenery south beyond them remain intact, attracting an endless stream of tourist buses to Kanóni. The islet in the foreground—linked to the mainland by a causeway—is the site of the convent of Vlachérna. A little farther out is Pondikoníssi, better known as **Mouse Island**, where a second chapel lies hidden beneath the cypress trees. You can hire a boat to visit this island, which some people believe to be the mythical Phaeacian ship turned to stone (see page 126).

A restaurant and bar on the hill provide a relaxing terrace from which to enjoy the view. Another pedestrian causeway across the lagoon leads to the small resort of Pérama.

The Achílleion Palace

Described on occasion as an architectural monstrosity, the **Achílleion Palace** stands out as the most controversial sight on Corfu—and one of the most popular (it is usually teeming with tour coaches).

The palace's romantic past as an imperial hideaway is no doubt part of the attraction. The beautiful Empress Elisabeth of Austria, wife of Franz Josef, fell in love with this site near Gastoúri on a visit to the island during the 1860s. Thirty years later, the

The statue of dying Achilles in the lush Achilleion gardens.

desperately unhappy Princess Sissy (as she was more familiarly known), stifled by the pomp of Vienna and stricken by the death of her only son, looked back with longing to her earlier experiences. In 1890, she purchased the land and commissioned the building of a palace that would be worthy of the Greek hero Achilles (hence the palace's name). The result, built in the Neo-classical style of the late 19th century, struck a number of observers as a most infelicitous hodge-podge.

The empress spent as much time as she possibly could at the Achílleion, staying there in utmost seclusion in the spring and autumn of each year. Poor Elisabeth only had a few years to enjoy her palace. Her tragic life came to a premature end in 1898 when, during a visit to Switzerland, she was mortally stabbed by an Italian anarchist. The Achílleion is a monument to this unfortunate monarch.

Up at dawn: Local fishermen in Benitses.

In 1907, Kaiser Wilhelm II of Germany acquired the palace, deeming it a suitable base from which to pursue his archaeological hobby. He made many changes, and proceeded to invite dignitaries from all over Europe to attend parties and concerts here. He also installed an awesome, 4½-tonne bronze, *Victorious Achilles*, by Johann Goetz, which looms 11½m (38 feet) high at the far end of the gardens.

The Achílleion was used as a military hospital in World War I. It subsequently became property of the Greek government, and from 1962 to 1983 it was leased out to a German company, which converted the opulent upper floors into a casino. In the 1990s, after renovation and the removal of the casino to the Hilton, the palace was opened to the public.

The Achílleion is adorned both inside and out with a flurry of pseudo-classical statues—Greek gods, goddesses, and heroes fill every corner. Note the statues surrounding the Peristyle of the Muses to the side of the palace, which are copies of originals in Rome's Villa Borghese gardens. Among all the statues scattered about the grounds, however, only one is considered by experts to have the slightest artistic merit—the dramatic *Dying Achilles*, by German sculptor Ernst Herter.

Inside, the garishly painted grand staircase leads to exhibition rooms on the first floor, while the ground-floor rooms house original furnishings and memorabilia of the Empress and the Kaiser. (One curious attraction is the adjustable saddle on which Wilhelm used to sit while writing at his desk.)

The palace's small chapel contains a fine rendering of Christ before Pontius Pilate, on the dome above the altar. Below it, the Virgin Mary rises out of the sea in *Stella del Mare* (Star of the Sea), a painting that was commissioned by Elisabeth following a dream she had in 1895.

The extensive grounds are perhaps the true highlight of the Achílleion. Its manicured hilltop gardens are a real pleasure, with magnificent sweeping views over the island.

The South Coast

Business is always booming in **Benítses**, 12½ km (7 miles) to the south of the capital—and that means "loud"! The resort is hugely popular with young foreigners who thrive on the lively nightlife and seemingly non-stop music, sleeping off the previous night's excesses on the rather diminutive strip of pebble beach. It's thought that Benítses may have been a holiday centre as far back as the time of the Romans;

A tranquil stretch of seashore near Boukári where the sea on this undeveloped beach is shallow and warm.

behind the harbour square stand the remains of what was once a Roman bath house, together with some floor mosaics.

For a brief respite from the nightlife, the northern end of town, near the old harbour, has pretty cottages that retain the character of the original fishing village, while the emerald valley at the back of the town is criss-crossed with footpaths in unexpected wilderness. A small museum in town offers opportunity for tranquil contemplation of treasures from the sea.

The busy coastal road continues as far as the twin resorts of **Moraítika** and **Messongí**, lying at the mouth of the Messongí River, 20 km (12 miles) to the south of Corfu Town. Despite an increasing amount of development now spreading back from the extensive narrow beaches, you can still find a traditional atmosphere in the old villages here. Remains of a Roman villa have been found at Moraítika, the busier and livelier of the two, while Messongí boasts some of Corfu's oldest olive groves, planted by Venetians over 500 years ago. The hills are great for walking.

The main road now curves inland, but you can follow the small track (seldom marked on the maps) that runs along the coast southwards of Messongí. Along this green and peaceful shore you'll find a few small tavernas where you can soak up the tranquil bay view. This pretty stretch leads to the small fishing village of Boukári.

Before returning to the main road at Argirádes, try another detour by following the signs to the little fishing village of **Nótos**. The timeless landscape of lush vineyards and stone cottages dotted between olive trees ends at a secluded cove, with a pleasant taverna above.

At the town of Argirádes, whose old monastery sports a striking Venetian belfry, head south across Corfu's tapering tail. This is olive, orchard, and vegetable country, and the island's principal wine-producing region. The dusty, sleepy villages here are brightened by masses of flowers and an occasional enthusiastic paint job. Women riding their donkeys, dressed in traditional Corfiote costume, are a common sight.

Another 10 km (6 miles) on, you will be funnelled into the long main street of **Lefkímmi**, the hub of this working agricultural region. The road now winds past narrow streets and squares, old town houses, and several churches to the Bailey bridge at **Potámi**, which straddles a picturesque canal lined with colourful caiques. A left turn just over the bridge takes you to **Boúka**, an undeveloped sandy beach where the sea is shallow and warm. A few trees around the small beach bar offer the only shade.

Kávos, 6 km (4 miles) on at the end of the main road, rivals Benítses as Corfu's "party" resort. Development has mushroomed in recent years, with a profusion of apartments, hotels, and well over 100 discos, bars, and restaurants flourishing incongruously on this remote tip of the island. Young crowds flock here in July and August, sometimes gaining a reputation for rowdiness. That said, the soft, sandy beach extending for 3 km (2 miles) is very shallow, and popular with families earlier in the season.

There's a variety of watersports available here, as well as boat excursions to Paxí, Antípaxi, and Párga (see page 70). A walk through peaceful country leads to Cape Asprókavos, on the island's southernmost tip, and the derelict monastery of Panagía Arkoudíllas.

Returning to Corfu Town, bypass the turn-off for Messongí and the coast, and carry straight on towards Strongilí. This route takes you inland through the pastoral scenery of the Messongí river valley before ascending the slopes of Corfu's second-tallest mountain, the 576-meter (1,889-foot) Ágii Déka. From **Ágii Déka** village—meaning "ten saints" —there is a spectacular view out to sea, overlooking Benítses and the far Kanóni peninsula.

THE NORTHEAST

The Northeast has some of the island's most stunning coastal scenery, and several busy and popular resorts. For many visitors, this part of Corfu, bulging out towards Albania, has a special appeal. Here lie the limpid aquamarine coves and rugged green mountain slopes that so entranced English author Lawrence Durrell. The inland area is crowned by Mount Pantokrátor, at 906 meters (2,972 feet) the highest peak on the island.

North from Corfu Town

The villages of **Kondokáli** and **Gouviá** lie within a sheltered lagoon about 8 km (5 miles) from Corfu Town. They are set off from the main highway and linked by a small road, with side tracks leading to sand and pebble beaches and a marina.

Gouviá, named after the bay on which it stands, is somewhat the smarter and more developed. Across the pretty bay you can see the little church of Ipapandí (Michaelmas), which juts out on a stone spit. Beyond is the island of Lazaretto, which formerly housed a quarantine station.

The extensive harbour has become an international marina lined with attractive yachts. It was once a Venetian naval base, and you'll find the skeletal arches of an old Venetian arsenal and shipyard at the end of Gouviá's beach.

All around the island you'll see signs advertising **Danília Village**, which lies just inland from Gouviá. This model Corfiote village was

A typical street in the model Corfiote village of Danília.

constructed by a local family, and incorporates all the different styles of architecture typical of the island. There's a church, a café, and an interesting folk museum containing a selection of antique farm implements and household goods, including a birthing chair and a rather unusual personal wind extractor. Craftsmen produce handmade items—from olive-wood artefacts to wildflower perfumes—which are sold in the shops under the arcades. The village is most spectacular at night, as coachloads of tourists arrive for the meal and floorshow of Greek folkdancing and singing that is usually held around the large main square (see page 82).

The resort of **Dassiá**, whose name means "forest," is backed by dense olive groves lying between the main road and the sea.

There's no central village, but only a string of restaurants, shops, and bars along the highway, with side roads leading down to the beach. The sand-and-shingle beach is long, narrow, and often crowded, but what it lacks in space it makes up for in its exciting array of watersports. There are numerous clubs providing waterskiing, jet skiing, and parasailing from the long piers jutting out into the bay, and the stream of colourful parachutes launching off jetties and criss-crossing in the blue sky is always a thrilling sight. Should you prefer a less strenuous form of activity, two large hotels have sunbathing areas set in beachfront gardens, which you can use for a small fee.

Small-boat excursions that will take you farther along the coast operate from Dassiá (and other major resorts). Alternatively, you can wander inland, on an uphill journey leading you past quiet villas and olive groves, as far as the art gallery housed in an old Venetian villa at Káto Korakiána.

Time for a peaceful dip at Ipsos beach and a glimpse of the surrounding cliffs of Mt. Pantokrátor, just north of Corfu Town.

Ípsos and **Pyrgí**, situated on a wide, beautiful bay about 15 km (9½ miles) north of Corfu Town, are surrounded by agricultural land and the sheer cliffs of Mount Pantokrátor. Together, they have been dubbed "the Golden Mile" by the innumerable armies of young singles who tend to congregate in the pandemonious discos and bars of this resort during the high tourist season. The extensive narrow beach that curves around the bay is a mixture of sand and shingle and offers an excellent selection of watersports facilities.

In times past Ípsos Bay was a target for Turkish raiders. Locals will tell you that the name Ípsos, meaning "height," was supposed to dissuade the Turks from mounting one of their attacks, while the name Pyrgí, "tower," probably derives from watchtowers built to warn of imminent raids. The resorts themselves are recent creations, however, and grew up around resettlements of villagers from Ágios Márkos in the hills above, whose homes were destroyed in landslides during the 1950s.

The tranquil old village of **Ágios Márkos** (St. Mark), accessible via a signposted road just outside Pyrgí, is worth a detour for its glorious views of the coastline and its two fascinating churches. At the top of the village is the 16th-century church of Christ Pantokrátor, with walls that have been completely covered by frescoes. The church is kept locked, but ask in the village and you may find someone willing to show you around. Lower down, the 11th-century Ágios Merkoúrios is Corfu's oldest Byzantine church, the only other one to be found on the island being Saints Iáson and Sosípatros in Corfu Town (see page 41). The church here also features ancient frescoes.

Mount Pantokrátor

Just beyond the Ágios Márkos turn-off, another road takes you up to the summit of **Mount Pantokrátor**. Round a series

of corkscrew bends, you'll be greeted by stupendous views over Ípsos Bay, just below the colourful village of Spartílas. The road broadens out into a rolling landscape of fruit trees, assorted fields, and vineyards, where some of Corfu's finest wine is produced. At Strinílas there's an inviting bar and café beneath a large elm tree. From this point, continue following the signs to Mount Pantokrátor.

The various hilltop monasteries around the island offer a gentle change of pace.

The paved road ends abruptly, becoming a rutted, gravel track increasingly difficult to traverse in an ordinary vehicle. You may then decide to abandon the car and walk, though the lack of shade trees can prove daunting in the afternoon summer heat. Even with sturdy transport, the final stretch to the peak is extremely steep, rough, and slippery, and it's advisable to make the ascent on foot. At the top, you'll be rewarded with unbeatable views: the entire sickle outline of Corfu and, over the narrow channel, Albania with its mysterious Lake Butrinto. To the south, in the blue Ionian, lie Paxos and distant Cephalonia.

The mountaintop monastery, which shares the summit with a rather unsightly aerial complex, was constructed during the 17th century on the site of an earlier church which had been built by neighbouring villagers in 1347. It is now unoccupied, except during the annual festival of the Transfiguration on 6 August (see page 90). However, you can help yourself to the water from the well.

The Northeast Coast

The dramatic beauty of northeastern Corfu begins above the bay of Ípsos and ends near Kassiópi, a lovely drive over a winding but good road, 20 km (12½ miles) long. This climbs sharply into the steep, green slopes that guard the coast, offering tantalizing glimpses of the sea below. Little of this shoreline can be seen clearly from the corniche road, but at various points it is possible to go down for a swim. It's obviously best, however, to explore by boat, which can be arranged from most jetties (see page 126).

At sea level, olive groves shelter a long, pebbly, and popular beach at **Barbáti**. Pretty **Nissáki**, where the water is a melodious medley of greens and blues, has perhaps the finest non-sand bathing on the island, making the steep descent to its beaches worth the effort.

Lawrence Durrell's beloved white house still stands at the peaceful pebble-bottomed bay of **Kalámi**. It has been partly converted into a taverna, from which you can enjoy the marvellous landscape that inspired him to write *Prospero's Cell* in 1939 (a largely evocative holiday read that describes Corfu in the days before tourism). Despite a number of vacation villas, a few restaurants, and a popular marina, it remains a tranquil resort, with swimming possible off the rocks, and a white pebble beach.

Charming **Kouloúra**, on the neighbouring bay, is scarcely large enough for a handful of fishing boats and a small taverna, but is one of the most picturesque corners on the island. Gerald Durrell, the brother of Lawrence, lived in the area as well and penned, for his own part, the amusing *My Family and Other Animals*.

Nestling beneath the hills —Ágios Stéfanos Bay

Just beyond is a viewpoint where you can gaze across the channel at Albania, which is a mere 2½ km (1½ miles) away. Before sweeping political changes, any fishing boats or innocent tourists who ventured even a few metres into Albanian waters were unfailingly challenged by armed patrol boats. Fortunately this is no longer the case, and you are now free to pay a visit to this formerly closed country at your leisure, while holidaying on Corfu (see page 74).

Another beauty spot awaits at **Ágios Stéfanos**, which also faces Albania 2 km (1 mile) off the principal highway among the northeast headlands. Fishing boats and yachts bob lazily in the circular harbour, ringed by whitewashed cottages and tavernas. Along one side there is a narrow pebble beach with shallow water, but beach shoes are recommended to give protection against the sea urchins that lurk in the rocky bottom. Although with each new year this enchanting resort becomes less of a secret, the laid-back atmosphere of a timeless fishing village still prevails.

The highly popular resort of **Kassiópi**, which lies 36 km (22 miles) from Corfu Town, was a thriving settlement in Roman times, visited by the Emperor Nero, Cicero, and

Cato, among others. It rivalled Corfu Town in importance in the Byzantine years. The Angevins built the now-ruined medieval fortress in the 13th century, on the site of an earlier castle, to provide protection against any barbarian raiders. The Old Fort was destroyed by the Venetians in order to prevent their Genoese rivals—or the rebellious locals—from seizing it and using it to their advantage.

The village is named after the god Kássios Zeus, protector of the remote corners of a land. The village church supposedly stands on the site of a temple which was built in his honour. The delightful Church of Panagía Kassiopítissa (Our Lady of Kassiópi) used to be the foremost shrine on Corfu before the arrival of St. Spyrídon; icons attest to the many miracles performed.

While today the town and the red-roofed villas surrounding the bay are increasingly packed with tourists during the summer peak, the horseshoe-shaped harbour is still home to local fishermen who carry on their business in the customary manner. Nightlife is lively, and four pebbly beaches allow for bathing and watersports in the small but attractive rocky bays.

Beyond Kassiópi the scenery alters. Softer, shrub-covered foothills border a broad coastal plain blessed with an abundance of hayfields, vines, and almond trees.

The North Coast

The shores of the north coast boast Corfu's longest unbro-

An artisian in his wood-working studio in Danília.

ken expanse of golden sand, which stretches from Róda to Acharávi and beyond.

Naturalists will be interested in a detour up the northern slopes of Mount Pantokrátor to **Old Períthia**, reached by a left turn some 6 km (4 miles) past Kassiópi. Outside of Loutses the road deteriorates, and the trek is best continued on foot. On the half-hour walk to this nearly-deserted mountain village you'll come across hundreds of butterflies, birds, and wildflowers. Overgrown footpaths between the crumbling old stone houses and churches provide a haunting glimpse of Corfiote life in the 1700s.

From the main highway, a number of side roads go down to a few relatively quiet, undeveloped beaches. Farther on is **Acharávi**, one of the fastest-growing resorts on the island, with all the usual facilities, but which is still less packed than other tourist destinations. The long, wide, sandy beach has warm, shallow water and good swimming farther out.

The neighbouring resort of **Róda** is more heavily developed. Its narrow, sandy beach (which joins Acharávi) is shallow for a long way out, making it popular with families. The remains of a fifth-century B.C. Doric temple, possibly dedicated to the god Apollo, have been discovered here.

THE NORTHWEST

The northwestern corner of the island rises again into mountainous terrain. Rugged cliffs drop sharply to the sea, creating idyllic coves and secluded beaches that you can only get to by boat. Footpaths along the precipices give dramatic views of the rocky western shore.

 The Northwest Coast

The booming resort of **Sidári**, 39 km (24 miles) from Corfu Town, is the most developed along the northwest coast. The

broad, sandy main beach has very warm, shallow water with a wide range of watersports. Sidári's finest feature, however, is the striking rock formations that rise out of the sea at the western end of the resort. The striated sandstone here is continually carved by the wind and the sea into sandy coves with caves and ledges (some of which are very good for diving). The most famous formation is the Canal d'Amour. Legend has it that any woman who wades or swims through this narrow channel when the water is in shade will win the man of her dreams.

From Sidári, boat trips run to the three small islands lying northwest of Corfu. Mathráki, Erikoússa, and Othoní, famous for their fishing grounds, have a total combined population of close to 1,000,

Where the cliffs meet the sea: Perouládes is a dramatic scenic spot.

*Pedalos are perfect for exploring sea caves
and grottoes on the island's west coast.*

though the limited tourism they now enjoy is bringing back
emigrants.

Stunning views of the northwestern tip of Corfu await at
Perouládes, 2 km (1 mile) on. Bear right at the end of the
village, following the signs to the Sunset Taverna. At the end
of the track, a flight of steps leading down to a remote beach
reveals a breathtaking view of sheer, gold-gray cliffs of striated clay plunging to the water, bordered by a delightful
fringe of deep, dark sand. There are no facilities on the beach
itself, but the Panorama Restaurant and Bar at the edge of the
cliffs provides a fantastic place to watch the sunset. From the
village, you can follow a footpath out to Cape Drástis, the island's northwestern tip, where you'll discover a pretty cove
and some interesting offshore rock formations.

Ágios Stéfanos, also called San Stefano and not to be confused with the eastern village of the same name (see page 56),
is a developing resort with a long, wide beach of densely
packed sand and pebble. It is popular with windsurfers and

still relatively uncrowded. A path leads out onto the headland, which is the most westerly point of both Corfu and Greece.

Another 45-minute walk to the south by the clifftop leads to **Aríllas** in the next bay. This low-key resort is smaller and slightly prettier than many developments, and has an attractive, sandy beach that shelves gently into the sea.

The tranquil village of **Afiónas** sits on top of Cape Aríllas, which forms the northern arm of Ágios Geórgios Bay. If you follow the path from the village square as far as Taverna Dionysos, you'll be greeted by a panoramic view of the bay's magnificent setting, ringed by green hills that are covered in olive and cypress trees.

From here you can follow a footpath out onto the cape. It leads down to an isthmus separating two tiny shingle beaches, which have been associated with the twin harbours of the Phaeacian palace in Homer's *Odyssey* (see page 13). The shallow, rocky shoreline is good for snorkelling. The walk is fairly steep but takes less than half

---

Orthodox Architecture

The most common type of church on Corfu is the single-nave basilica, which is divided into three parts. After lighting candles at the entrance, the congregation sits at the back, men to the right side, women to the left. The middle part of the church is raised and separated by a railing. Ceremonies such as weddings and baptisms take place here. The large screen where the icons stand, called the iconostási, separates the third part.

Three doors lead to this holiest part of the church, which always faces east. The middle door, or king's gate, guards the altar, where the communion bread and wine are prepared. Women are not allowed to enter. The balcony actually constitutes a fourth part: the women's gallery, where, in times past, women were secluded, present but unseen.

an hour each way, though it's slow going on the narrow, rocky path between the dense, scratchy gorse; good footwear is a must. You can also reach these beaches by *pedalo* from Ágios Geórgios.

The marvellous, unspoiled beach of coarse sand at **Ágios Geórgios** (St. George) which stretches for 3 km (2 miles) along the bay, is among the most beautiful on Corfu. Windsurfing and other watersports are available, though the water is deeper and much colder than elsewhere on the island. Development is progressing, but for the moment its remote location keeps the crowds away.

Around Paleokastrítsa

You can reach the most celebrated beauty spot on the island by a fast, paved road from Corfu Town, 25 km (15½ miles) away. **Paleokastrítsa** used to be a favourite picnic spot for the High Commissioner, Sir Frederick Adam, and his Corfiote wife, and in the 1820s he had a road built across Corfu to reach it (after first building a military hospital here to justify the expense). Once you see it, you may well agree

The spectacular shore off the main beach at Paleokastrítsa is a wonderful sight to soak in.

that it has some of the loveliest scenery in the entire Mediterranean.

Six small coves with incredibly clear turquoise water nestle in a coastline of hills and promontories draped in olive, cypress, and lemon trees. Strips of partly sandy, partly shingle beach ring the shoreline, and sea grottoes yawning out of sheer cliffs invite exploration.

Many claim Paleokastrítsa was the site of King Alcinous's fabulous palace—the magnificent setting is certainly worthy of Homer's effusive prose (see page 13). Out to sea, a big graceful rock called Kolóvri is said to be the Phaeacian ship that once bore Ulysses home. Even sceptics have to concede that Kolóvri does resemble a ship. Oblivious to the rock's mythological significance, sea birds now lay their eggs on it, in nests sheltered by a sturdy, cactus-like plant called *frangosikiá*.

Paleó, as it is often called, was never a village itself, but just the port of the hilltown of Lákones. The year-round population is slightly under three dozen, but this is hard to believe during the high season, when several hundred Corfiotes move down from their hillside homes to cater for the hordes of visitors who jam its hotels and villas.

No building has been permitted to crowd the bright little **monastery** that perches on the main, wooded promontory. Constructed during the 13th century after the discovery here of an icon of the Virgin Mary, it was rebuilt following a fire in the 17th century; the monks' cells, now empty, were added then. The church has a charming Ionian bell tower in the local fashion, with three bells representing the Holy Trinity.

A tiny museum harbours ancient icons, vestments, and the like, together with some enormous bones (probably whale) extracted from the sea early last century. You can also see an

Visitors from all around the island come to enjoy the main beach at Paleokastrítsa.

old olive press and the huge wine barrels used for crushing grapes by foot.

Entrance to the monastery is free, but a donation is expected. Remember to dress appropriately (bathing costumes are not acceptable).

Paleó's main beach is the most crowded, but from here you can take boat excursions to Corfu's only sea caves and grottoes, with their mysterious pink rocks and blue "eyes"—extremely deep holes which, with the play of sunlight, turn an incredibly deep blue colour.

During the high season, Paleokastrítsa is best in the early morning or early evening, as then the crowds and the jarring sounds of engines give way to the chirping of birds and the quiet whoosh of surf on shore.

The finest view at Paleó is from a lookout point set high above the coastline. A narrow asphalt road twists up through olive groves to the precariously perched village of Lákones. A little farther on, at a café called—with some understatement—"Bella Vista," is a magnificent **panorama**, one of the finest in Europe. All of Paleokastrítsa, the amazing shoreline, and even Corfu Town are visible. Paleó's coves fan out below: from left to right, Agía Trias, Platákia, Alípa, Ágios Spyrídon, Ágios Pétros, and Abeláki. The first three cluster together in a cloverleaf shape, forming a larger bay.

Looking down, you see the monastery jutting dramatically over azure water—a superb location. If King Alcinous didn't put a palace there 3,000 years ago, he certainly should have!

From Paleokastrítsa, which means "the old castle," you can see the massive walls of **Angelókastro**, the medieval fortress constructed by the despot of Epirus in the 13th century. In 1537, several thousand Corfiotes held out against Ottoman attack in this impregnable citadel. Today, you can climb to the summit and explore the ruins from the village of Krini. Look out for the cave chapel of Agía Kyriakí, with hermit cells which have been carved out of the rock, as well as traces of frescoes.

Continue on to **Makrádes**, where the main road is lined with souvenir shops and tavernas catering to the tour coaches. Some of the locals may run out into the road and flag you down, hoping to sell you wine and herbs. Luckily, this ambitious brand of salesmanship is not commonplace around the remainder of the island. The village itself (off a side road to the left) is a bright, whitewashed cluster of houses with many picturesque corners.

If you have a good vehicle, just beyond Makrádes you can follow the steep, gravelly secondary road, which is rutted in parts, to **Pagí**. The first reward is a stunning vista over Ágios Geórgios Bay before you get there. The second is the timeless mountain village itself, crowned by an Ionian belfry.

Alternatively, you can continue along the main road as far as Troumbétas Pass (troumbétas means "trumpet"); during construction of the road to Paleó, the officer in charge used to stand on the pass above and blow his trumpet to call the men to lunch. From here you have various options—double back to Pági and Ágios Geórgios via Arkadádes, head north to Sidári or Róda, or return to Corfu Town via Skriperó.

Compellingly beautiful, too, is the half-hour boat trip from Paleokastrítsa to Ágios Geórgios Bay. You chug along past jagged cliffs which dwarf your bobbing outboard, while peeking into mysterious sea caves and looking out for the dolphins that often cavort in these waters. Rounding the edge of the bay, you're very likely to come across a fishing boat or two working nets. The area is known for rewarding catches, and you may find extremely fresh fish available at the modest eating places here.

Just below Paleokastrítsa is the large, attractive bay of Liapádes, your first glimpse of the sea when arriving by road. Although it's best explored by boat, simple tracks lead to the partly sandy, summarily developed **Géfira** beach, where you can swim in what the Corfiotes call their "green waters." There is a glorious setting of cypress trees all around.

THE WEST COAST

The wide Rópa Valley separates Paleokastrítsa from the central and southern beaches of the west coast. This former marsh was drained by the Italians during their brief occupation in World War II, and is now the island's agricultural heartland. You'll be treated to many glimpses of rural life in the fields and farmyards when driving across the pretty plain.

Farther south down the west coast lie some of Corfu's best beaches, with wide stretches of deep, golden sand. Some are blissfully under-developed and take a little effort to reach.

The Rópa River flows down through the valley and out to the sea at **Ermónes**, making it yet another contender for the *Odyssey* legend (see page 13). Situated on a bay about 16 km (10 miles) from Corfu Town, it has a small beach of shingle and pebble. The whole setting is dominated by a hillside hotel.

Nearby **Myrtiótissa** is described by some enthusiasts as the most beautiful beach in Europe. Sheer cliffs covered with trees and shrubs drop directly to the sand, creating a sense of wonderful isolation. At both ends of the long beach curl

Most roads are lined with souvenir shops.

rocky promontories offering marvellous snorkelling in crystal-blue water.

This enchanting beach completely vanishes from time to time. During the winter, when high waves pound the shore and torrents of fresh rainwater plummet from the cliffs, the sand is carried out to sea. It invariably returns with milder tides, but the size of the beach varies from year to year.

Maps seem to be deliberately vague, and only one sign to the monastery, in Greek, advertises Myrtiótissa. It's about an hour by foot from the nearest bus stop on the Pélekas-Vátos road, and car or scooter travellers will only get part of the way along the rough dirt track through the olive groves. If you're lucky, peasants will direct you; otherwise, take the second right along a winding turn-off from the main road.

The other way to reach this beach is by boat. Excursions from Paleokastrítsa, Ermónes, and Glyfáda have swelled the number of bathers here, and its solitude is not as it was.

Myrtiótissa is unofficially recognized as the island's nudist beach. Nude bathing is tolerated at Pélekas beach also, which has excellent swimming conditions, a long, sandy shore, and a couple of tavernas. Despite poor access down a very steep, rutted road, it can get very busy in high season.

The Southwest Coast

The town of **Pélekas**, popular with young travellers, perches at the top of a winding road and is today busy and commercial, full of travel agencies, restaurants, discos, and rooms to let. It is famous, however, for the Kaiser's Throne at the pinnacle, a panoramic viewpoint where the German emperor built a telescope tower to watch the spectacular sunsets.

A winding road from Pélekas drops down to **Glyfáda**. Against a backdrop of crumbling cliffs with rock formations at either end, this large, sandy beach is one of the finest and most popular on the island. Swimming is superb; the water is initially shallow, but deepens farther out, and there can be a strong undercurrent at the northern end (as on many beaches along the west coast). Swimmers must obey the safety flag if it is flying. Development at Glyfáda is growing, and the beach is frequented by daytrippers from Corfu Town and other resorts.

Scenic **Ágios Górdis**, surrounded by verdant slopes all covered with orchards, olive groves, and market gardens, is punctuated by a gigantic erect rock rising from the water at the southern end—an excellent spot for snorkelling and spear-fishing, as are the rocks at the northern end. Sadly this once-quiet spot, with its long sand-and-shingle beach, has become very crowded in high season, and inadequate parking creates chaos at the beach access. The Pink Palace, a resort overflowing with *ouzo*-sodden revelers, is a case in point. It remains to be seen whether this beautiful setting survives.

Be sure to visit the hill town of **Sinarádes**, taking time to wander through this charming village, with a Venetian church tower and picturesque, flower-bedecked houses round every corner. Past the central square, look for signs to the excellent **Folk Museum**. Housed in a traditional Corfiote house, its rooms are an authentic reconstruction of a village home of the last century. The proprietor explains how each item was used, and even demonstrates the delightful shadow puppets in the second-floor museum.

A second beach named **St. George** (Ágios Geórgios—see page 62), about 35 km (22 miles) south of Corfu Town, reached through pine woods and olive trees, is a popular destination in southwestern Corfu, and a far cry from its northern namesake. The huge beach, which stretches for several kilometres, has been aptly nicknamed "golden sands."

The northern end, where it is generally possible to find a peaceful spot of your own, is backed by gentle sand dunes. Behind them is the salt-water lagoon, Lake Korissíon, where both botanists and birdwatchers will find an unexpected wealth of wildlife to observe. The rather haphazard resort sprawls along a stretch in the middle, while the more developed and much busier "golden beach" to the south offer watersports.

The relatively new resort of **Agía Barbára** (not shown on many maps) lies farther south at the end of this long, sandy stretch. Beyond reach of public transport, the reddish-gold sand beach is often deserted and excellent for windsurfers.

You'll find Corfu kids take visitors in their stride,
happy to just relax and watch passers-by.

EXCURSIONS

While there's very little danger of developing "island fever" on Corfu, you may also want to visit the nearby mainland, Albania, or the idyllic island of Paxí, which are easily accessible. Corfu travel agents can provide you with information on day-trip excursions, and on ferry schedules if you wish to stay longer (see page 126).

☞ Paxí (Paxos)

One of the most delightful island experiences in the Mediterranean awaits you just 10 nautical miles south of Corfu. Paxí (Paxos), the smallest of the seven principal Ionian islands, starts its seduction even before your boat docks, with dark green hills and astonishingly clear aquamarine waters.

This tiny, verdant island—approximately 11 km (7 miles) long and 5 km (3 miles) wide —has some 300,000 olive trees and 1,500 permanent inhabitants. To this day it earns more from olives than tourism.

The mighty rock of Orthólithos stands as a sentinel over the sea caves of Paxi.

According to Greek mythology, the sea god Poseidon created Paxí by striking off the southern part of Corfu to make a retreat for himself and his beloved Amphitriti. Circe, the enchantress who in Homer's *Odyssey* detained Ulysses on her island and turned his men into swine, came from here.

Peaceful Paxí often appeals to those who want to get away from it all, though this can be exceedingly difficult in mid-summer, especially in August when it's a magnet for Italian tourists. Then, prices swell accordingly and accommodation is heavily booked. The island only has one hotel; most accommodation is in fairly upmarket villas and apartments, though visitors who only want to stay a couple of nights can often find rooms to let in private houses. As the daily ferries from Corfu Town don't return until the next morning, it's sensible to try to arrange accommodation in advance.

While Paxí is characterized by glorious greenness, its numerous streams dry up in summer and the island suffers an annual water shortage following the influx of vacationers. Visitors should therefore use water conservatively.

Boats arrive at **Gáios**, the small quayside capital of the island. The pretty waterfront square is lined with tavernas, shops, and charming weathered houses, while the handsome yachts of the marine jet-set fill the harbour. During the high season its narrow streets buzz with day trippers from passing cruise ships.

Across the narrow sea channel opposite Gáios is the islet of Panagía, which is crowned by a lighthouse and chapel. Islanders undertake a pilgrimage here each Assumption Day (15 August), returning to the town after the service for celebrations in the main square. On the islet of Ágios Nikólaos, which helps shelter the harbour from the open sea, you'll find the ruins of a 15th-century Venetian fortress.

Lákka, 8 km (5 miles) away, is a pretty port situated around a horseshoe-shaped bay on the northern shore of Paxí, and is ideal for watersports. It's the island's sailing capital, and has several pleasant cafés and tavernas, as well as an aquarium displaying all the local marine life. The tiny fishing village of **Loggós**, or Longós, huddled around a lovely harbour, lies between the two.

There is a regular bus service between the three main towns (Gáios, Lákka, and Loggós)—though this only operates during the day and early evening. Taxi and scooter hire is available, but note that it can be difficult, if not impossible, to find a taxi late at night.

Paxí's clear, limpid waters are irresistible. The island has no sandy beaches, though off the shingle strip at Lákka the bottom is pure sand. However, you'll find excellent swimming from flat rocks and numerous pebbly coves around the shoreline, even if many are secluded and accessible only by boat. There's a small strip of sand on the islet of Moggoníssi in the far south, but it is always crowded.

Walking around the island itself is sheer delight. Timeless tracks along stone terraces and through mature olive groves end in idyllic hamlets. Some 80 churches, rarely used nowadays for lack of priests, nestle in the trees. Along the roadsides you'll come across abandoned stone cottages and fine old olive presses, as well as lovingly tended grape arbours, cactus, and bougainvillaea in profusion, while the surrounding hillsides are dotted with round, stone towers of ruined windmills missing their sails.

Signs:
ΙΔΙΩΤΙΚΗ ΠΛΑΖ- Private Beach; ΑΠΑΓΟΡΕΥΕΤΑΙ ΚΟΛΥΜΠΗΣΗ- No swimming

A popular walk leads from Magaziá, in the centre of the island, up to the tidy hilltop cemetery at the Ágii Apóstoli (Holy Apostles) church, where there is a striking view of the chalk-coloured Erimítis cliffs. Between Magaziá and Fontána stands the island's largest olive tree—it takes five men with outstretched arms to embrace the huge twisted trunk. This giant stands in an incredible grove of 500-year-old trees, all still producing fruit faithfully every two years.

From Lákka there are some pretty walks to a lighthouse on the cliffs and, somewhat farther afield, as far as the hilltop monastery of Ipapandí, where a delightful bell tower provides scenic views.

Even on the briefest visit, be sure not to miss the truly spectacular **sea caves** in the towering cliffs along the west coast. From your boat, you may not be able to spot the seals which have for so long inhabited the cavernous depths, but you will see blue water that is totally dazzling in intensity.

Snorkelling or scuba diving here is something you won't forget. The sea depth off these sheer rocks plunges from 25 to 90 meters (27 to 98½ yards), with fish of varying sizes gliding along in schools at different levels.

The largest of these caves, Ipapandí, was said to be Poseidon's home. A modern legend relates that a Greek submarine hid here during World War II, venturing out on occasion to conduct its valiant operations. Soaring out of the sea along this stunning coast you'll also notice the massive hulk of Orthólithos—a huge finger of rock that has been hewn out of the cliff face by the elements.

A boat trip around the island (very worthwhile) can be easily arranged from either Gáios or Lákka. Alternatively, you can negotiate a price for a private tour with some of the operators. Small-boat hire is also available, but the rough sea conditions of the west coast can only be attempted safely in a larger vessel.

From Corfu Town, there is at least one public transport boat as well as hydrofoil to Paxí each day during the tourist season. The journey takes anywhere from 1½ to 3 hours. There are also one-day excursions to Paxí and neighbouring Antípaxi, several of which visit in addition Párga on the mainland (see page 77). In the high season there is a daily caique service between Gáios and Párga, approximately 90 minutes away.

To really enjoy Paxí, you should plan to spend around two nights—enough time to see the island's highlights and have a swim on Antípaxi. Beware, however: there's a compelling charm about the place, something in the relaxed atmosphere which has led countless visitors to linger far longer than they intended.

☞ Antípaxi (Antipaxos)

For the finest beaches in the area, take a day trip to **Antípaxi** (Antipaxos), a completely unspoiled island 3 nautical miles to the south of Paxí. (By caique the journey from Gáios takes 30-40 minutes.)

Cloaked in vineyards, lapped by transparent turquoise water, Antípaxi is occupied by only a handful of permanent residents but attracts plenty of visitors who converge on the island's two beaches. Vríka has an arc of fine, white sand in a little cove, with tavernas at either end and a few beach umbrellas for hire. The nearby bay of Voutoúmi has brilliant white stones along its coastal strip, but a soft, sandy bottom underwater. Apart from one taverna on the hillside, there are no facilities.

Swimming at both Vríka and Voutoúmi is superb, but don't expect to enjoy the idyllic setting in solitude. Excursion boats continually drop off increasing numbers of bathers throughout the day, while numerous private boats moor offshore. In high season, these sweet little beaches can be pathetically overcrowded.

☞ Albania

For the last half century, visitors to Corfu could only gaze across the channel at the mysterious land of Albania which lies, at its nearest point, a mere 2½ km (1½ miles) away. The Communist government which ruled the country since 1945 had virtually sealed its borders to foreigners. However, with the collapse of the Communist regime in 1991, Albania's isolation ended, and the next year its doors were opened to travellers waiting to explore this beautiful, undeveloped land.

Corfu is now one of the easiest access points for a first glimpse of Albania. Day trips operate regularly from Corfu Town to archaeological sites in the southern region.

On its 1½-hour crossing, the ferry plies between the scenic coastline of northeastern Corfu and the more barren hills along the shore

There are many comfortable villas for rent on Paxí.

of southern Albania. The many pillboxes squatting along the cliffs serve as a reminder of not-so-distant Cold War fears. Below lie enticingly deserted beaches.

The initial view of the port town of Saránda seems to confirm Western notions of Communism's drab, soulless style of architecture. In actual fact, the town is a former military point, hence the concrete buildings lining the shore. There are a few remnants of pre-World War II buildings inland, but most were destroyed by German bombing.

Several decades of self-imposed isolation have meant that the country's population of 3¼ million enjoys few modern conveniences. Roads are poor, transport erratic, restaurants and facilities few and far between. Outside the cities, the rural lifestyle belongs to a previous era: scattered, feudal-like villages cling to the edge of the mountains and to fierce clan loyalties. In spite of their hardships, however, the people here are warm, friendly, and generous to visitors.

Outside Saránda lies a beautiful terrain. Beyond a broad valley, part wild, part cultivated in former collective farms, looms the outline of rugged and foreboding mountains. The narrow, winding road makes for a bumpy ride, with drivers having to negotiate potholes or dodge the wandering goats and

Roman floor mosaics have been preserved in the baptistry at Butrinti.

cattle. If you're in need of a break, look for a roadside stop where locals sell sodas, beer, watermelon, and cherries kept cool in a bubbling stream.

The tour visits the ancient city of **Butrinti**, which lies on the southern shore of the great Lake Butrino. It is reached via a corniche road that skirts the lake, revealing glimpses of the citrus and olive country on the peninsula below.

The area was first inhabited in prehistoric times, and Butrinti is thought to have been founded by Pelasgians, predecessors of the ancient Greeks. It remained a thriving city well into Roman times.

The buildings of this 11-hectacre (27-acre) site are well preserved, sprawling over a lush, shady landscape. A defensive wall of large Cyclopian stone blocks encircle the hilltop, and forms the oldest surviving part of the fort. A theatre, temple, promenade, and the Lion Gate date from the third and fourth centuries B.C. Beginning in the first century B.C., the Romans greatly expanded the city, and constructed a new gymnasium, public baths, and a baptistry. Exquisite floor mosaics, covered over by sand for protection, accent the baths and baptistry.

Butrinti thrived as a city in the early Middle Ages, becoming a strategic pawn, much like Corfu, in the power battles of the Byzantine and Venetian eras. At the end of the 18th century it was captured by the fearsome despot Ali Pasha, whose ruined castle still lies today at the outlet of the Vivari channel. Deserted by 1850, Butrinti then fell to the forest, which enclosed it until its rediscovery in 1922.

A number of tours also visit a unique beauty spot named the **Blue Eye**. Here, amidst a serene, wooded grove, an underground spring so deep it has never been measured bubbles to the surface, emerging in a magical pool of irridescent blue. Legend has it that the 12-headed dragon, Kulcedra, jealously guarded the spring and held back its waters from the villagers, who were required to sacrifice young maidens on the spot. As if to corroborate the story, flitting around the pool are dozens of blue dragonflies, the same shimmering colour as the spring.

The price of the tour usually includes the fee for your visa which the tour company (see page 115) arranges. Remember that you will need to bring along your passport.

Párga

Párga is a pretty village on mainland Greece's northwestern coastline. It has started to fall prey to developers, but for day trips or for a longer stay, it is still a delight. Its hospitable people, the whitewashed houses, and casual cafés and tavernas convey a charm slightly different from Corfu's.

Párga's picturesque harbour is approached through its little offshore islands rising out of a semicircular blue-green bay. One of these, tiny Panagía Island, is crowned by a church.

A Venetian castle looms above on the promontory. The climb up Párga's steep streets to the fortress is actually shorter than it looks from below, and is well worth the effort for the stupendous views over the town and the sparkling sea. Be sure to follow the path around the crest of the hill for a look at the high-walled ruins and for further great views of the next bay.

Oxen and Omen

The name Butrinti derives from an ancient legend. Prince Aeneas, sailing west from Troy, sacrificed an ox to ensure his safe entry to Epirus. The wounded ox suddenly plunged into the sea, swam into a bay, and struggled ashore, where it fell and died. Aeneas took this as an omen and called the place Buthrotós, after the wounded ox.

The main town beach is predictably crowded, but Párga also offers splendid swimming at two long sand-and-pebble beaches, north and south of town, Líchnos and Váltos. The water is clear and steeply shelved. Spear fishermen and snorkellers have all kinds of rocky depths to plumb nearby, and you can easily find fishermen to take you out in small boats for good catches. Alternatively, hire a *pedalo* to paddle around the islets.

A popular boat trip from Párga travels up the Acherón, thought to be the mythological **River Styx**, gateway to the underworld. You can also visit the hilltop **Necromantíon**, the Oracle of the Dead accessible only by car or taxi. Here, in an underground chamber, the ancient Greeks—under the auspices of Hades, the Lord of the Underworld—sought contact with the souls of the departed.

Párga is teeming with travel agents who can help you find a room at one of the many small hotels or in a private home. Among the groves of olive, orange, and lemon trees, there's excellent camping as well.

Albania's magical Blue Eye: it's depths are unknown.

A ferry runs between Párga from Corfu Town twice a week. At other times, you need to catch a boat to Igoumenítsa, 48 km (30 miles) north, but good connections can be made between the Corfu ferries and buses. Alternatively, there are daily cruise ships that spend a couple of hours at Párga before going to Paxí, returning in the evening to Corfu Town.

WHAT TO DO

SHOPPING

Your best bet for finding traditional souvenirs in Corfu is to head straight for the shops in and around the historical centre of Corfu Town. For a wide variety of quality items, you can also try Danília Village, near Gouviá, where craftsmen make items by hand, using traditional methods.

Prices are on the increase in Greece, and you shouldn't expect to get a great deal in the way of bargains on Corfu. In souvenir and gift shops, you'll find that a

> **Items marked ΕΚΠΤΩΣΕΙΣ are on sale.**

bit of good-natured bargaining is tolerated—many of the owners are multi-lingual, so you'll have no difficulty communicating. Bear in mind, however, that local profit margins have to cover not only the tourist months, but also the off-season, when the shop is closed. Nevertheless, your chances of a discount will improve substantially if you buy more than one item.

Remember that because Greece is a member of the E.U. many goods will incur the value-added tax of about 18%.

Best Buys

Gifts from the olive tree: Corfu's most plentiful commodity —its olive trees—provides the basis for many fine souvenirs. Local artisans carve a variety of attractive bowls, trays, and oddments from olive wood. However, there's more than wood to the venerable trees. The island's olives and high-quality olive oil are appreciated worldwide.

Pottery, glass, and ceramics: Corfu is home to numerous talented potters and crafts people. You'll come across some lovely ceramics, including museum copies. Many shops here display various symbols of Greece mounted on brilliant-blue

blown glass. One of the most popular of these is the "eye," which is hung as a decoration in homes to ward off evil spirits.

Gold- and silversmithing: Gold and silver are both good buys. Silversmiths still create bowls and trays using the old patterns of their Greek and Venetian ancestors, beating out the silver much as they would have done centuries ago. Many of the jewellery designs are based on traditional forms that reflect the development of Greek civilization, including such classic symbols as the lion, dolphin,

Handcrafted baskets are one of the many great finds on a shopping spree in Corfu.

ram, and bull. Shop around when buying jewellery, and be sure to use a reputable jeweller. Gold and silver are sold by weight—each item should be weighed in front of you—while any workmanship and creativity involves an additional cost. Some gold rings are made from two different purities—before you buy, check for hollowness, and make sure that the correct weight-price equivalents are being used.

Leather: Leather goods such as handbags, sandals, wallets, and belts are also good buys in Corfu Town. (Pantón Street is home to many young and creative fashion designers.) While mainland Greece is the centre of the fur industry, you will also see coats and jackets for sale on the island.

Weaving and embroidery: You'll discover an over-whelming array of handwoven and embroidered items. Colourful woollen shoulder bags called *tagári,* handwoven floor mats of wool and small carpets (the best come from Epirus), tablecloths, napkins, aprons, skirts, and blouses of lace and cotton (in particular those woven in Corfiote villages) are al-ways popular. There's no better buy in this category than cotton needle-work shawls and bedspreads; these

> Sizes can vary. Be sure to try on clothing and shoes before you buy.

must usually be ordered, and are mailed without fail to your home address. The town of Kassiópi is home to a traditional industry of lace and crocheted goods, and is a good place to buy such items.

Other Specialities

Kumquat liqueur is a speciality made from small Japanese oranges that are grown on the island. There are medium and dry varieties of this sweet, orange-coloured drink, though the clear-coloured extract is considered the best quality. It is sold throughout Corfu, and the Ameco factory on the Paleokastrítsa road is a popular stop with tour groups. You can also sample kumquat in the form of crystallized fruits.

Another particularly sweet treat worth trying is **nougat** of almonds or sugared nuts. In addition, the richness of the island's flora ensures that its famous **honey** always possesses a distinctive character.

Corfu has its own **wine** producers, and you can purchase a number of local vintages on the island. Other drinks available include **oúzo,** the national drink, and Greek **brandy.** All are reasonably priced.

Other typically Greek souvenirs include a strand of worry beads *(kombolóïa),* tapes or CDs of Greek folk songs, skewers for *souvlákia*—often elaborate—and *bríkia,* long-stemmed Turkish coffee pots.

ENTERTAINMENT

Corfu's night-time entertainment begins with the vólta, the evening stroll. It's best along the Listón, where you can linger over a drink in the French-style cafés while watching the parade of young Corfiote boys and girls, respectable couples, double-skirted women pushing grandchildren in prams, and smartly dressed families. This is the place to be seen for Corfu's young and old alike.

Music and Dance

Corfiotes' love of a good song and dance runs deep. At traditional tavernas or at "Greek nights" organized by places such as Danília Village, a meal includes a floor show of Corfiote music and dancing. Many bars and hotels offer smaller-scale Greek nights.

The *sirtáki* is Greece's best-known group dance, which can easily sweep up everybody in the taverna. It is great fun, but not considered a totally serious dance by Corfiotes: the steps aren't that difficult to master, even after a few drinks!

Other steps are much more challenging. You'll see the island's own two splendidly intricate dances, the *agiriótikos* and the *gastouriótikos.* Both of these involve 15 or 20 women joining hands, forming a circle, and enclosing two or three men who twirl and leap agilely to the music of an accordion, a guitar, and a fiddle. This trio of instruments produces the most typical of Corfiote music.

Traditional Corfiote and national Greek dances (such as the circular *kalamatianós* and *tsakónikos)* are taught at an early age—not hard to believe when you see the dancers' precise and fluid movements.

The *zeibékikos,* always a crowd pleaser, is performed by a man or pairs of men. The spectators, clapping in time to the music, cheer on the dancer who bends back and seems to pick up a table with his teeth. (If you watch closely, he's actually taking the table's weight on his chest and stomach.)

Women or young girls alone do the lively, whirling Ágios Geórgios dance, particularly on village feast days. You're also likely to see the traditional Greek butchers" *chasápikos,* which is similar to the sirtáki, and the wildly energetic sailors' dance, the *naftikós.*

All these dances are usually accompanied by the famous eight-stringed mandolin, the *bouzoúki,* which for many foreigners has become—inaccurately—synonymous with all Greek music. The instrument, which is of Turkish origin, is a comparatively recent import to the island, though the haunting melodies of Mános Hadjidákis and Míkis Theodorákis form an intrinsic part of Greek—and Corfiote—folklore. If a taverna has no live bouzoúki player, it will play the recorded stuff!

Spend an enjoyable evening filled with lively traditional Corfiote music and dance.

Corfu is a musical island. Corfu Town alone boasts 15 philharmonics, representing in all more than 750 musicians, as well as a municipal choir and a chamber music group. Marching bands are a regular fixture at festivals, and Sunday concerts often take place during the summer at the bandstand on the Esplanade.

You'll see the most authentic performances of folk songs and dances at village festivals throughout the season, where young and old alike participate, dressed in the traditional costumes of their ancestors.

Bars and Nightclubs

Corfu Town's discos are located in the Emborikó Kéndro (commercial centre) along the main road to the north of the port. Here you'll find popular establishments such as Sax,

Greek Easter

No more colourful Easter *(Páscha)* celebration occurs anywhere in Greece than on Corfu. Here it's often called *Lambrí,* meaning "brilliance." Throngs of Athenians and other mainlanders flock over to watch. Every church has its Good Friday procession. The best starts after nightfall from the cathedral with the bishop, dignitaries, and Corfu's famous town bands.

On Holy Saturday morning the patron saint, Spyrídon, is paraded at length around town with spectacular pomp in honour of his miraculous intervention in 1553 which saved Corfu from famine. Then, at 11am, police clear the main streets and suddenly pottery, old plates, vases, and anything else that will shatter is hurled from the upper storeys of houses. The old Corfu custom is supposed to show anger at Judas's betrayal of Christ.

At midnight, when the bishop intones *Christós Anésti* (Christ is Risen), every electric light goes on, fireworks soar overhead, church bells ring, and, most memorably, everyone lights a candle. Easter has arrived. On Easter Sunday all are invited to the local naval base and some police stations; wine flows ceaselessly and men do the traditional Greek and Corfiote dances.

Bora-Bora, and Apocálypsis—which boasts a swimming pool. All the major resorts around the island have at least a few bars and discos. Benítses, Ípsos, and Kávos together share the reputation for the island's wildest nightlife, with music round the clock.

Casino

Corfu's casino (tel. 36540) is housed at the Hilton Hotel in Kanóni, and opens from 8:00 P.M. until 2:00 A.M. Games offered are roulette, blackjack (21), baccarat, and chemin de fer. You can choose from paying a single-entry fee or purchasing a weekly ticket. Take your passport along. Men are required to wear jackets and ties.

Cinema

Corfu Town's outdoor and indoor cinemas show foreign films, sometimes of recent vintage, with original soundtrack and Greek subtitles. Most of the films are English, French, or American. The Pallas is located on G. Theotóki Street and the Phoenix, an outdoor cinema, is on Marasli.

You can try practically every watersport that has been invented at the popular Dassiá.

SPORTS

With Corfu's marvellous climate, it's certainly possible to stay outdoors ten or twelve hours every day of your holiday. One important piece of advice, however: the sun can be treacherous—it bakes white skins crimson in an amazingly short time, and that's just as true under a light cloud cover or haze as under clear blue skies. Use high-factor lotions or total block, and try to avoid staying too long in the sun. Quite aside from sunbathing, there's a wealth of recreational activities to offer.

Swimming: The island's sometimes rocky, sometimes sandy, now flat then hilly coastline offers every setting any swimmer could desire.

As a general rule, Corfu's western and northern shores tend to have more surf than the eastern coast, which faces the mainland, while the best sandy beaches front on to the open Ionian. Until mid-summer, the water at Paleokastrítsa and at other western swimming areas is cooler than on other parts of the island. Corfu's beaches are among the cleanest in Europe, and only at or around Corfu Town (most notably at Garítsa Bay and the port areas) should swimming be avoided on account of pollution.

Signs:
ΕΙΣΟΔΟΣ - entrance
ΕΞΟΔΟΣ - exit

The only beach area with lifeguards is Mon Repos. Always take care while swimming, and pay attention to the warning flags on some western beaches (red or black if currents or breezes are strong).

Sunbathing and swimming in the nude are considered to be punishable offences, though toplessness is common in the island's tourist resorts.

A large number of hotels have swimming pools. In theory, you can use any hotel pool (except for the most deluxe) if you rent a sunbed, patronize the pool bar, and don't bring in your own food or drink. Signs are usually posted stating the policy of the hotel.

Snorkelling and diving are excellent among the island's innumerable rocky inlets, and you'll find some fascinating small sea grottoes and offshore rocks along the west coast. Don't be put off by eel grass at certain east-coast points; some of the most colourful fish lurk in these shallows.

Corfu's coastal waters are deep and clear, allowing divers some superb views. Scuba-diving schools—most notably the ones at Paleokastrítsa and Ípsos—have qualified instructors who will choose dive locations according to the amount of experience you have. Extended boat trips are available for advanced divers. You will need a health certificate (obtainable from a Corfu doctor) before you can enroll at a scuba-diving school. For the more advanced trips, or to go by yourself and rent equipment, you will need to be able to show a diving certificate.

Fishing is unrestricted around Corfu, and the abundance of fish ensures that even the most novice angler will come away with a catch. You don't need a licence, and you can readily hire equipment and a boat on the quayside, or strike a deal with local fishermen who will often take small groups out on fishing trips.

On the east coast, look out at night for the *gri-gri*—two large boats pulling a number of small crafts festooned with lamps to attract the fish.

Boating: Undoubtedly the best way to enjoy the coastline is by boat. You'll find everything from *pedalos* and banana boats to yachts for hire on Corfu, by the hour, the day or the week.

You can rent all categories of motorboats, from a small five-horsepower outboard to a 10-metre (33-foot) caique with an inboard motor and two crew members. Rates vary according to size. Several harbours offer dinghies for private hire by the week at remarkably reasonable prices.

Greece's only glass-bottomed boat, the Kalypsó Star, is stationed in Corfu Town's Old Port. A popular tourist attrac-

Boats of all sizes are for hire on Corfu's coastal waters.

tion, it leaves every hour for a 50-minute trip around Vido Island, where caged sea lions perform for the passengers.

Sailing and yachting: Yachting is one of the most popular sports on Corfu. You can charter a sailboat or motor yacht, with or without a crew, though you need to show a proficiency certificate from a recognized yacht club. The Corfu Yacht Club offers training courses for beginners. Flotilla cruising is also available, and is best arranged from home, through a specialized tour operator.

Corfu Port is a class "A" yachting station, with dockside supply facilities for water, fuel and provisions. It is one of the few designated "entry-exit" ports in the country, where the obligatory transit log for every yacht may be obtained. This permits free sailing throughout Greek waters. Elsewhere on the island, Gouviá possesses a large, lovely marina with several hundred berths. Paleokastrítsa is the west-coast port.

Watersports: Corfu has numerous schools where you can learn to waterski. Avoid the northern shore, however, as the winds here can be too strong. Boards and sails for windsurfing are available for hire at nearly every beach on the island where the right conditions prevail, and tuition is offered at many places. Parasailing has become incredibly popular, and is available at several beaches, as is jet-skiing.

You'll find some major watersports centres to the north of Corfu Town. In Dassiá, ski clubs like Corfu Ski Club and Ski Club 2001 offer a wide range of sports from their long piers, while Ípsos beach provides similar facilities. Water-skiing and windsurfing are also available at all major hotels on the island.

Rowing clubs exist all around Corfu. Many offer water polo as a sideline. If you would like to participate, try approaching the Nautical Club of Corfu in Garítsa Bay.

Golf: The highly acclaimed Corfu Golf Course (tel. 94220) is situated not far from Ermónes beach in the Rópa Valley. The 18-hole course here, 6 km (4 miles) long with a par of 72, is likened to a links course, with water hazards and a design that provides a real challenge for seasoned golfers. Fairways are kept lush by an automatic watering system.

The course attracts golfers from hotels all over the island. You can arrange lessons with qualified pros — though it's best to book ahead — and clubs and other essentials are available for hire. There's also a good pro shop and club-house with a bar and restaurant.

Tennis and squash: If your hotel doesn't have courts, try the Corfu Tennis Club at 4 Romanoú Street in Corfu Town (tel. 37021). Founded in 1896, the club is the oldest of its kind in Greece. It has four asphalt courts which you can rent by the hour. Visitors are welcome during the morning from 8:00 A.M. until noon. There is a more recently established club called Coryfó in the suburb of Kefalomándiko. Lessons and racquet hire are available at both clubs, as well as at many of the hotels that have courts.

The Corcyra Beach Hotel in Gouviá (tel. 30770) has squash courts and racquet rental. You must book in advance.

FESTIVALS AND HOLY DAYS

1 January: St. Basil's Day *(Protochroniá)*—children and traffic policemen receive presents; strangers may be offered a sprig of basil.

6 January: Epiphany *(ton Theofaníon)*—the Bishop blesses the waters by throwing a cross into the sea; boys dive to retrieve it.

25 March: Greek Independence Day procession in Corfu Town.

Carnival: Parades and festivities during the last days of Carnival.

Orthodox Sunday: Litany procession of the holy relic of St. Theodóra Augusta.

Clean Monday: First day of Orthodox Lent *(Katharí Deftéra)*—in good weather everyone goes out for a picnic.

Palm Sunday: Litany procession of St. Spyrídon's remains.

Easter: Good Friday-Easter Sunday—major celebrations (see page 84). Easter Monday: festival at Lákones. First Friday after Easter: festival of *Zoodóchos Pighí* (life-giving spring) at Paleokastrítsa.

21 May: Ionian Union Day *(Énosis ton Eptaníson)*—marks the anniversary of the seven islands joining Greece in 1864.

July: Local festivals—26 July at Benítses and Avliótes, 8 July at Kávos, 20 July at Makrádes, Magouládes, and Ág. Prokópis.

August: 1-6—Festival at the Monastery of Pantokrátor. First fortnight—music, dance and arts in Káto Korakiána.

11 August: Feast day in honour of St. Spyrídon in Corfu Town.

15 August: Assumption Day—festival in Kassiópi in memory of the Virgin Mary.

23 August: Festival of the Madonna *(Odighítria*—"our leader")* at Pélekas; also festival at Gastoúri.

8 September: Festival of the Virgin at the village of Áfra.

24 September: Festival of the Virgin Myrtiótissa near Glyfáda and at the village of *Vátos*.

November: St. Spyrídon Day *(Agíou Spirídonos)*—all of Corfu's Spíroses receive gifts on their name day; on the first Sunday in November, the saint's body (see page 35) is stood upright in church so that people can kiss his feet.

Horseback riding: There are a number of riding centres on the island, and both beginners and experienced riders can enjoy Corfu's beautiful countryside on horseback. A good place to try is Kerkyra Golf Hotel (tel. 31785), just north of Corfu Town; in summer you need to book a day in advance.

The Rópa Valley Riding Stables (tel. 94220) are located near the golf club and offer 1- to 2-hour rides in the beautiful Rópa Valley. There are also stables at Róda, Gouviá (tel. 30770), and Kassiópi, and the Barrique Riding Stables (tel. 52143) at Áfra, in the centre of the island.

Hiking and Walking: You can climb Corfu's tallest peaks, Pantokrátor and Ágii Déka, or any of the rather less challenging hills on the island. Otherwise, there are many footpaths and mule tracks, some several hundred years old, which lead to olive groves, woods, meadows, and rustic villages. During springtime the landscape is blooming with wildflowers.

Should you leave the track, be careful not to walk over any olive nets. If you are hiking overland rather than along the road, be sure to wear a good pair of boots, as the terrain is rocky in parts and there are a variety of snakes, though most of these are harmless.

Climbing and biking: One of the island's newer activities is rock climbing, and there are facilities available at the Corfu Climbing Club (tel. 39481). The club offers training for beginners, as well as trips to some of the challenging rock faces on Corfu for more experienced climbers.

You can rent mountain bikes at resorts. If you would rather join an organized tour, contact the tourist information office (see page 124) for a list of specialized bike tour operators.

Cricket: Throughout the season, matches take place regularly upon the Esplanade in Corfu Town on Wednesday, Saturday, and Sunday, usually attracting a number of enthusiastic spectators. Corfu clubs frequently play against visiting teams

Catching those rays at poolside: kids are welcome almost everywhere on the island.

from Malta and Britain, among others. Vacationers who wish to participate should enquire through their hotel receptionist about arrangements, or telephone 42542 for further information about organizing play. It may be possible to play with one of the Corfu teams.

CHILDREN'S CORFU

Corfu is a popular holiday spot for families, and most resorts are happy to cater for kids. Many larger hotels have separate, shallow children's swimming pools and play areas, and some of the large, class-A hotels have special games and activity programmes for kids.

While most beaches are perfectly safe for children, those with sandy shores and very shallow water may be most appealing to families with very young children. These include Róda, Sidári, Acharávi, Aríllas, Bouka, and nearby Kávos, though the latter is also known for its gregarious nightlife (see the cover of the guide for more beach briefings).

In Corfu Town, kids usually enjoy a ride around town in the colourful 19th-century horse-drawn carriages, while an ice cream on the Listón always goes down well. They will certainly like the Shell Museum (see page 34) and the Kalypsó Star (see page 87). In Paleokastrítsa, a boat trip to the caves and grottoes can be very exciting.

EATING OUT

Excellent natural ingredients are at the heart of most Greek cuisine. Delicious grilled fish, spitted meat, crisp Greek salads, and exquisite fruit have good, fresh flavour, and you can dine in a pleasant outdoor setting. Greek cooking is simple, and at times imaginative, using a few basic ingredients and herbs for flavouring. Olive oil, lemon, tomatoes, onion, garlic, cheese, and such herbs as oregano feature in the many Greek specialities.

Within cosmopolitan Corfu Town, as well as in the resorts, you can find everything from gourmet cuisine through Chinese fare to hamburgers and pizza. With so many restaurants and tavernas around, you won't want to be confined to a full-board plan at a hotel.

In most Greek restaurants it is common practice for customers to enter the kitchen and inspect the array of pots and pans on the stove. Once you have decided exactly what you would like, just point it out. A half-portion is *olígo* (a little). Alternatively, ask for a menu (which is usually printed in at least one major European language in addition to Greek). You can then attract your waiter's attention by calling out *parakaló!* (please).

Meal prices do vary, but in general they are less expensive than in most of Western Europe. Government price controls operate for all

> **Blue telephone booths are for local calls only; orange ones must be used for all other calls.**

categories of restaurant in the country except deluxe.

The service charge is included in the bill, but diners normally leave between 5 and 10 percent extra with the bill for the waiter, as well as a few drachmas on the table for the youngster who usually brings the iced water or an ashtray or cleans off the table.

Greeks generally wish each other "bon appetit" before beginning a meal. In Greek, the expression is *kalí órexi*!

Starters

Mixed appetizers (*mezédes*) are nearly always a popular choice with both Greeks and visitors. Be sure to try some of these Corfu favourites:

> Before ordering you can stroll into the kitchen and have a look at what's cooking.

Dzadzíki: a yoghurt dip with crushed garlic and grated or finely sliced cucumbers. It is served chilled, generally with other mezédes and bread.

Taramosaláta: spread made out of the roe of grey mullet (cultivated in Corfu's Korissíon lagoon) which, together with mashed potatoes, olive oil, lemon juice, or sometimes moistened bread, is beaten into a smooth, pink paste. Greeks eat it on bread chunks or on lettuce as a salad.

The Claw's the Thing

Menus all over the island will have you believe that *astakós* is a kind of lobster, but while *astakós* looks like the noble crustacean—and is priced accordingly—it is, in fact, not lobster but saltwater crayfish, meaning it's clawless.

You may see lobsters flexing their distinctive claws at a few restaurants on Corfu, but *astakós*—billed as "Mediterranean lobster"—are far more likely to appear on the menu.

The crustacean scene is further confused by *karavída*, which is a similar but bonier variety of astakós, said to be more tender than other kinds. You should, however, pay much less.

If you do find the real thing, you'll often be shown the creature moving its appendages, to prove it's alive. Your choice is weighed in front of you, because you pay by the kilogram. Expect a very large bill at the end of your meal!

Corfiotes, aghast at prices today, have been known to remark: "At these prices you don't eat the lobster; he eats you!"

Dolmádes: grape leaves that have been stuffed with minced meat (often lamb) and/or rice and then seasoned with grated onion and herbs. Often they are served hot accompanied by an *avgolémono* sauce (chicken stock, lemon, and eggs).

Taste Corfu's specialty dishes at one of the many cafes.

Kalamarákia: small squid, usually fried in batter, and then served with lemon.

Maridákia: whitebait, generally fried and flavoured with a dash of lemon.

Greek Specialities

Saláta choriátiki: Eaten as a starter, separately, or with main courses, this "village salad" is ubiquitous throughout Greece and is simply known as "Greek Salad." Tomatoes, sliced cucumber, onions, and sometimes green peppers are topped with a little white *féta* cheese and black olives. You may want to mix up your own olive oil and vinegar as an accompaniment.

Moussaká: one of the most popular of all Greek dishes. Alternate layers of sliced aubergine (eggplant) and minced meat are baked with a white sauce and grated cheese.

Pastítsio: minced meat and macaroni pie with white sauce and cheese, eaten as either a first or main course.

Fish and Seafood

Fresh fish abounds, but even so, restaurant prices are likely to shock many visitors. A genuine seafood speciality on the island is the pleasantly piquant *bourdétto*: white fish—which should be either *skorpiós* or *skilópsaro*—stewed in hot red

A laterna player entertains patrons seated on the Listón.

pepper and olive oil, nothing more and nothing less.

There are several varieties of fish that have no English translation, such as the tasty *melanoúri* or *sargós*, usually simply grilled and served with a dash of lemon. *Barboúni* (red mullet), a Mediterranean favourite, is probably the most popular fish on Corfu. Some others are: *fagrí* (sea bream); *garídes* (prawns), occasionally served Greek style—cut up and simmered in a spicy tomato sauce with olives; *glóssa* (sole); *sinagrída* (red snapper); *xifías* (swordfish); *gávros* (anchovies); *soupiés* (cuttlefish); *sardéles* (sardines); and *oktapódi* (octopus).

Meat Dishes

Soffríto: a speciality of the island—slices of beef or veal stewed in a sauce of garlic and wine vinegar with a touch of black pepper.

> Vegetables are usually eaten cold (raw or boiled, and then cooled), or tepid.

Stifádo: another speciality of Corfu —beef stewed with baby onions in a finely spiced tomato sauce.

Pastitsáda: beef stewed in a richly flavoured tomato sauce, served with pasta.

Kokorétsi: spiced sausages of innards and herbs.

Souvlákia: skewered veal or lamb grilled over charcoal; it may also go under the name of *shish kebab*.

Keftédes: Greek version of meat balls, made from minced beef or lamb, flavoured with grated onion, spices, and herbs.

Arní frikassé: lamb stewed with green vegetables.

Kotópoulo: chicken, usually served roasted, most deliciously on a spit over charcoal.

In addition, you'll generally find steaks and chops; some outdoor restaurants specialize in grilled meat and salad.

From Eggs to Honey

Anywhere on Corfu or indeed in Greece for that matter, the lowly omelette (*omeléta*) always makes a good choice—whether plain, or with cheese, ham, or onion.

Among the island's seasonal and delectable vegetables are *angináres* (artichokes), which may be served *laderés* (in oil) or as part of a stew, *fasólia* (butter beans), and *fasolákia* (string beans).

The magnificent wild strawberries (*fráoules*), which appear in May and June, may be the tastiest treat in the Ionian. Corfiotes have a national passion for nuts: *foundoúkia* (hazelnuts) are outstanding.

The cheese scene is rather uninspiring, though you will come across a pleasant Swiss-type Gruyere (*graviéra*), an interesting sheep's milk cheese (*kefalotíri*), and, of course, *féta*—goat's milk cheese steeped in olive oil and brine.

Sweets are just that—and usually sticky as well. *Mandoláto*, an almond-and-honey nougat, has a big following, as does the famous *baklavá*, flaky and paper-thin *fíllo* pastry, filled with chopped almonds and walnuts and finally drenched in honey or syrup. Corfu's honey (*méli*) rates very high on the list, and makes a wonderful breakfast snack poured onto the island's superior yoghurt (*giaoúrti*).

Drinks

If you order **coffee**, you may well be offered the traditional Greek brew, *ellinikó*—a thick, strong concoction, boiled to order in a long-handled copper or aluminium pot called a *bríki* and poured, grounds and all, into a tiny cup. Traditionally, a glass of cold water is served alongside the coffee.

If you prefer instant coffee, ask for *nes* or *neskafé*—or say *kafé me gála* (milk coffee). Ask for *éna varí glikó* if you want yours sweet; *éna métrio*, medium, or *éna skéto*, without sugar. *Zestó* means hot, as opposed to *frappé*—iced coffee.

Tea (*tsái*) is usually good. Bottled **soft drinks**—notably lemonade (*lemonáda*) and orangeade (*portokaláda*)—are excellent here.

And, of course, Corfu is the only place in Greece where you can get genuine, 19th-century-style **ginger beer**. Locally given the name *tzinzerbíra* (pronounced "tsintsibeera"), it is served well chilled and is always extremely refreshing in the hot weather.

Lager-type **beer** is a very popular summertime drink on Corfu. A large number of well-known European brands are on sale here, bottled under licence in Greece.

> **Greek coffee: the beans are ground to a fine powder, boiled with water, and then poured, grounds and all, into a cup. Let the grounds settle, then drink half the cup.**

Oúzo, the national aperitif, is very often taken neat (*skéto*) on Corfu; when you add cold water it turns milky—and becomes rather less potent. *Oúzo* is distilled from crushed grape stems, and has a notably aniseed flavour. Olives, cheese, a bit of tomato, crisps, or chips, will often be served with your drink for a small extra charge. (Foreign aperitifs and liquors are available at much higher prices than Greek drinks.)

Corfu produces a reasonable quantity of local **wine**, but most of this is kept by the vineyard owners for their own private drinking. Usually light red (*kokkinéli*) or deep purple in appearance, it is best drunk cool from the cellar, where it sits in wooden casks. If you are fortunate, as you wander around the inland villages you might find some on sale in the *kafepantopoleíon* (coffee bar and grocery store). A number of restaurants also stock it; ask for *krasí heéma*.

Among local bottled wines, the rarest and most expensive is *Theotóki*, a dry white wine produced solely from grapes cultivated in the Rópa Valley. For everyday drinking, choose among the *Kastelláno*, *Karpó*, *Corifó*, and *La Dame* wines.

There is also a vast range of mainland Greek wines to choose from. Three top-class reds are *Cáva Tsántali*, *Cáva Boutári,* and *Calligás Montenéro*. Those who prefer white or rosé might try Tsántali's *Agiorítiko* and *Macedónian* brands or *Boutári lac des Roches*, which is a smooth white. At the cheaper end of the spectrum are brands such as *Deméstica* and *Rotónda*, as well as the reliable table wines produced by the companies named above. At the end of a meal, *Mavrodáphne*, a sweet red similar to Marsala, is well worth a try.

Wines which are marked "Appellation of Origin" on the label have been made from grapes harvested in a controlled region and are almost always excellent. Among these are the burlap-wrapped white *Robóla* from Cephalonia and the red *Náoussa*.

Retsína, an acquired taste, is less popular on Corfu than elsewhere in the country. But you'll have no trouble finding this inexpensive pine-resinated white wine. Originally, Greek wines were all transported and

A winemaker presses grapes at a local winery.

stored inside pine-wood casks sealed with resin. Later, when vats and bottles replaced the casks, the Greeks continued to resinate their wines to obtain this special flavour. Much *retsína* today is chemically aged, however, and an instant resin flavour is added without assistance from the old-fashioned pine barrels.

The Ionian islands are well known for their liqueurs. The speciality of Corfu is *koum kouat*, a syrupy confection that is produced from miniature oranges, which grow here, far from their native Japan.

As for mineral **water**, the Corfu varieties are usually flat, not bubbly. Tap water is automatically served everywhere, but is best avoided (see page 128).

One common toast while drinking is *stin igiá ("ya") sas*! meaning "to your health!" A reply to any toast, in the sense of "the same to you," is *epísis*.

To Help You Order

Could we have a table? **Tha boroúsame na échoume éna trapézi?**

I'd like a/an/some ... **Tha íthela ...**
beer **mía bíra**
mineral water **metallikó neró**
(iced) water **(pagoméno) neró**

bread	**psomí**	napkin	**petseta**
coffee	**éna kafé**	potatoes	**patátes**
cutlery	**macheropírouna**	rice	**rízi**
dessert	**éna glikó**	salad	**mía saláta**
fish	**psári**	soup	**mía soúpa**
fruit	**froúta**	sugar	**záchari**
glass	**éna potíri**	tea	**éna tsäï**
icecream	**éna pagotó**	milk	**gála**
meat	**kréas**	wine	**krasí**

INDEX

Acharávi 58, 92

Achilleion gardens 45

Achílleion Palace 44-45

Agía Barbára 69

Agía Kyriakí 65

Agíi Déka 50, 91

Ágios Geórgios 61-62, 65, 69, 83

Ágios Górdis 68

Ágios Márkos 53

Ágios Merkoúrios 53

Ágios Spyrídon 36, 64

Ágios Stéfanos 56, 60

Ágios Stéfanos Bay 56

Agía Barbára 69

Agía Kérkyra 42

Albania 9, 14, 50, 54, 56, 70, 74-75, 78

Ancient City 13, 18, 42-43, 76

Angelokastro 16

Angevins 16, 57

Antípaxi 50, 73-74

Archaeological Museum 14, 38-39, 43

archaic lion 38, 40

Argirádes 49

Aríllas 61, 92

Baptistry at Butrinti 76

Barbáti 55

Benítses 47, 49-50, 85, 90

Blue Eye 76, 78

Boukári 48-49

Boúka 49

British Cemetery 41

Buthrotós 77

Butrinti 76-77

Byzantine Museum 32-33, 38

Campiello 31, 36

Canal d'Amour 59

Cape Asprókavos 50

Caves of Paxi 70

Chalikiópoulos lagoon 44

Constantinople 15, 18, 32, 35-36

Corcyra 13-14, 18, 40-41, 43, 89

Corfu Reading Society 32

Corinth 14, 18, 40

cricket pitch 27, 29

Danília Village 51, 79, 82

Dassiá 38, 51-52, 85, 89

David Gower 29

Douglas, Sir Howard 41

Durrell 10, 50, 55

Edward Lear 10

Emmanuel Tzanés 32, 42
Empress Elisabeth 23, 45
Epirus 16, 18, 65, 77, 81
Erikoússa 59
Ermónes 13, 66-67, 89
Esplanade 27-31, 37-39, 84, 91

Faneroméni 35
Folk Museum 51, 68

Gardiki 13
Gastoúri 45, 90
Gáios 71-74
Géfira 66
Glyfáda 67-68, 90
Gorgon pediment 38, 40
Gouviá 17, 50-51, 79, 88-89, 91
Greek National Art Gallery 38

Hadjidákis 83
Homer 8, 10, 13, 61, 63, 70

Ionian Bank 34, 38
Ionian Monument 27
Ionikí Square 34

Kalámi 55
Kanóni 13, 42-44, 50, 85
Kapodistríou Street 32, 37
Kardáki Spring 13, 43
Kassiópi 55-58, 81, 90-91

Káto Korakiána 38, 52, 90
Kávos 49, 85, 90, 92
Kerkyra 91
Kim Hughes 29
Kolóvri 13, 63
Kondokáli 50
Kouloúra 55
krasí 99-100
Krini 65

Lake Korissíon 69
Lákka 71-73
Lefkímmi 49
Lepanto 17-18
Liapádes 66
Loutses 58

Magouládes 90
Makrádes 65, 90
Messongí 48-50
Mon Repos 13-14, 42-43, 86
Moraítika 48
Mount Pantokrátor 30, 37, 50, 53-54, 58
Mouse Island 13, 44
Mt. Pantokrátor 52
Museum of Asiatic Art 28, 38
Mussolini 24

Necromantíon 78
New Fortress 33-34
Nissáki 55

Old Fort 15, 17, 26-27, 29-31, 57
Old Períthia 58
Orthodox cathedral 36
Orthólithos 70, 73
Ottomans 17, 19, 32

Pagí 65
Palace of St. George 27, 38
Palace of St. Michael 27, 38
Paleokastrítsa 13, 16, 21, 62-67, 81, 86-88, 90, 92
Pantokrátor 30, 37, 50, 52-54, 58, 90-91
Paper Money Museum 34, 38
Paxí 7, 24, 33, 50, 70-75, 78
Paxos 54, 70
Párga 50, 73, 77-78
Pelasgians 76
Perouládes 59-60
Pélekas 67-68, 90
Potámi 49
Prince Aeneas 77
Prokópis 90
Pyrgí 53

River Styx 78
Roman Catholic cathedral 39
Rópa Valley 66, 89, 91, 99
Róda 58, 65, 91-92

Shell Museum 34, 38, 92

Sidári 58-59, 65, 92
Sinarádes 38, 68
Sinarádes Folklore museum 38
Sosipatros 40
Spianáda Square 29
St. Basil's 90
St. George 27, 30, 38, 62, 69
St. Jason 14, 40
St. John the Baptist 35
St. Spyridon 26
St. Theodóra Augusta 35, 90
St Iáson 14

Temple of Artemis 14, 38, 40, 43
Tha íthela 100
Theotóki Square 37
Tomb of Menecrates 38, 40-41
Town Hall 37, 39
Troumbétas Pass 65

Vátos 90
Venetian well 36
Vídos Island 24, 32

HANDY TRAVEL TIPS

An A–Z Summary of Practical Information

A Accommodation 105
   Airport 106
   Antiquities 106
B Bicycle and Motor-
   scooter Hire 107
C Camping 107
   Car Hire 107
   Climate and
   Clothing 108
   Communications 109
   Complaints 110
   Crime 110
   Customs and Entry
   Formalities 111
D Driving 112
E Electric Current 113
   Embassies and
   Consulates 114
   Emergencies 114
G Guides and Tours 114
L Language 115
   Lost Property 116
M Media 116
   Medical Care 117

   Money Matters 118
O Opening Hours 120
P Photography and
   Video 120
   Police 121
   Public Holidays 122
R Religious Services
   123
T Time
   Differences 123
   Tipping 123
   Toilets 124
   Tourist Information
   Offices 124
   Transport 125
   Travellers with
   Disabilities 126
   Travelling to Corfu
   126
W Water 128
   Weights and
   Measures 128
Y Youth Hostels 128

A

ACCOMMODATION (See also CAMPING on page 107, YOUTH HOSTELS on page 128, and RECOMMENDED HOTELS on page 129)

Many hotels are fully booked for the high season by package-tour operators, from mid-June until October, especially around the 15 August holiday (see page 122). Reservations are strongly recommended, but if you do arrive without one, try a travel agency in town or check at the information cantre at the New Port, just inside the Customs House. Offices of the Greek National Tourist Organization (E.O.T.) maintain a list of all Corfu hotels (see TOURIST INFORMATION OFFICES on page 124).

Prices are controlled according to a category list compiled by the EOT, based on the building's age, facilities, amenities, and other factors. Hotels are rated from A to E, but prices can vary widely in each category. Luxury establishments, rated L, are not price-controlled.

Categories C and above all have private bathrooms. In lower categories, rooms with bath are rare, though almost all rooms have showers. Price reductions are frequently offered for children. 10% is sometimes added to the bill if you stay only two nights.

Rates and all extra charges (such as hot water if your room has no private facilities) must, by law, be posted in your hotel room.

Villas. Corfu has more villas to let than many other Greek tourist centres—ask the Tourist Information Office for a current list. Accommodation ranges from cottages sleeping only two to lavishly appointed summer homes at monthly rates. Domestic help is sometimes included in the price. If arranging a villa from abroad, be sure to ask about accessibility to food shops if you'll be without transport.

Rooms in private homes are rented at usually negotiable rates and conditions. They are almost always clean, but you'll rarely have your own shower and toilet. Call the Association of Owners of Private Rooms in Corfu, tel. 26133, Monday-Friday 8am-1pm and 6-8pm in summer, for details of vacant rooms around the island.

Corfu

I'd like a single/double room.	**Tha íthela éna monó/dipló domátio.**
with bath/shower	**me bánio/dous**
What's the rate per night?	**Piá íne i timí giá mía níkta?**

AIRPORT (ΑΕΡΟΔΡΟΜΙΟ—*aerodrómio*)

Located only 1 km (1/2 mile) from the capital, Corfu's lagoon-side airport has a modern runway capable of handling all but the largest jets.

There are no porters, but carts are available for a small charge. If you can't see any in the arrival area, walk round to the check-in desks. For security reasons, charter luggage is not dealt with in bulk —charter passengers, like others, have to handle their own luggage.

The terminal building has a souvenir shop, car-rental desks, and offices of various travel agents (not for booking accommodation but for dealing with clients on arrival and departure). Newspapers are sold at the souvenir shop.

The currency-exchange office is open from 9am to 2am, if there are international flights scheduled to land at night. (It's a good idea to buy Greek currency before travelling, in case the office is closed.)

There is no bus service from the airport to Corfu Town or vice versa. Taxis, however, are inexpensive (about 1,500drs).

For general airport information, tel. 30180. For international flight information, tel. 38694. For domestic flights, tel. 38695. For lost and found in the airport, tel. 33576.

ANTIQUITIES (ΑΡΧΑΙΑ—*archéa*)

Antiquities may be exported only with the approval of the Greek Archaeological Service and on paying a fee. (The main Archaeological Service is in Athens; check with the Corfu tourist office for the local contact.) Anyone caught smuggling an artefact may get a long prison sentence and stiff fine, and the item will be confiscated. Travellers buying an antiquity should get the dealer to obtain an export permit.

B

BICYCLE and MOTORSCOOTER HIRE (ΕΝΟΙΚΙΑΣΕΙΣ ΠΟΔΗΛΑΤΩΝ/ΜΟΤΟΠΟΔΗΛΑΤΩΝ — *enikiásis podiláton/-motopodiláton*) (See also DRIVING on page 112)

You'll find rental agencies at the airport and in all the tourist centres. Rates vary, so it's wise to shop around. Agents charge a non-negotiable insurance fee for all motorized two-wheelers. If you hire a motorcycle, insist on a crash helmet—it's against the law to ride without one. Inspect brakes, tyres, etc., before hiring, and drive with care.

What's the rental charge for a full day?	**Póso kostizi giá mía iméra?**

C

CAMPING (ΚΑΜΠΙΓΚ — *camping*)

Camping in Greece is only permitted on organized sites. There are 15 official, organized campsites on the island. All sites have the usual facilities and are open at least from April to October. For a list, contact the EOT office in Corfu or your nearest Greek National Tourist Organization (see TOURIST INFORMATION OFFICES on page 124).

May we camp here?	**Boroúme na kataskinósoume edó?**
We've a tent.	**Échoume míaskiní**

CAR HIRE (ΕΝΟΙΚΙΑΣΕΙΣ ΑΥΤΟΚΙΝΗΤΩΝ — *enikiásis aftokiníton*) (See also DRIVING on page 112)

You'll find car-rental firms at the airport and throughout the island, especially in tourist centres. As throughout Greece, car hire is not cheap. Deposits are often waived for credit-card holders and members of large tour groups, who may also obtain a small discount. An International Driving Permit or a full national licence from your country of residence is required and must have been held for at least one year. Depending on the model and the hiring firm, the minimum age for renting a car varies from 21 to 25.

Third-party liability insurance is often included in the rate, and complete coverage is available for a modest extra charge. Enquire whether mileage is included in the rate or is charged in addition. All rates are subject to a stamp duty and local taxes. Though most firms take credit cards, they often charge 3-5% extra for using them.

I'd like to rent a car (tomorrow).	**Tha íthela na nikiáso éna aftokínito (ávrio).**

CLIMATE and CLOTHING

The months of July and August are the sunniest and warmest on Corfu—and attract the most tourists. You may prefer to stay between mid-May and late June or from early September to mid-October.

December is Corfu's rainiest month and January its coldest, but even during these mid-winter doldrums the climate is temperate. Spring, when Corfu bursts with wildflowers, is great for walking.

	J	F	M	A	M	J	J	A	S	O	N	D
air temp. °C	10	10	12	15	19	24	27	26	23	19	15	12
air temp. °F	50	50	54	59	66	75	81	79	73	66	59	54
sea temp. °C	15	15	15	16	18	21	24	25	24	21	19	18
sea temp. °F	59	59	59	61	64	70	75	77	75	70	66	64
daily hours of sunshine	5	6	7	7	9	10	11	12	9	6	4	3

Clothing. Unless you want to gamble at the casino (in the Corfu Hilton Hotel at Kanóni), you can leave ties and fancy dresses at home; clothing is almost always casual on Corfu. After dark, even in midsummer, you may appreciate a wrap, a jacket, or a sweater.

Since it does rain from time to time on Corfu, some sort of protective coat or an umbrella is a good idea—except at the height of summer. Choose lightweight cotton clothing in spring and summer, and a warm jacket, sweater, and rainwear in autumn and winter.

Sensible walking shoes are a must, especially heavy boots for cross-country hiking; plastic or rubber bathing slippers are useful for stony beaches (rubber-thonged sandals are sold on the island).

Mosquitoes can be a bother on Corfu, so bring along mosquito repellant. Alternatively, you can buy small electric devices that you plug in at night to keep the bugs at bay (available on Corfu).

COMMUNICATIONS (See also OPENING HOURS on page 120 and TIME DIFFERENCES on page 123)

Post Office (ΤΑΧΥΔΡΟΜΕΙΟ—*tachidromío*). Post offices handle letters, parcels, and money orders, but not telegrams and phone calls; they sell stamps. Look for a yellow sign reading ∂§.Δ∞. The main post office is at the corner of Alexándras and Megális, tel. 25544.

Registered letters and parcels to foreign destinations are checked before being sent, so don't seal them until you have presented them at the post office desk. Stamps are also sold at most places which sell postcards, though there's a small surcharge. Letter boxes are yellow. In tourist hotels, the receptionist oftens take care of dispatching mail.

Mail. If you don't know ahead of time where you'll be staying, you may address your mail poste restante: name, Poste Restante, Corfu GR 491-00, Greece. In Corfu Town, you can pick it up from the main post office. Take your passport with you for identification.

Telephones, telegrams, and fax (*tiléfono; tilegráfima*). The main Corfu office of Greece's Telecommunications Organization (O.T.E.), at Mantzárou 3, is open from 7am to 11pm daily. There is another branch on Kapodistríou, across from the Esplanade, open 8am-10pm. Here you can send telegrams and make phone calls—or have an operator obtain the number for you. International trunk lines are often busy and you may have to wait up to two hours at peak times. Reverse-charge (collect) calls can be made here from Monday to Friday (dial 151 for Europe and 161 for the rest of the world).

You can make a local call or long-distance and international calls from many coin- or card-operated phone booths. Coin phones accept 10-, 20-, and 50-drachma coins, and phone cards can be bought at kiosks and hotels. To call Corfu Town from outside the town, use prefix 0661.

Fax services are available from major hotels in Corfu Town.

Have you received any mail for ...?	**Échete grámmata giá ...?**
A stamp for this	**Éna grammatósimo giaftó to**
letter/postcard, please.	**grámma/giaftí tin kart postál, parakaló.**
express (special delivery)	**exprés**
airmail	**aeroporikós**
registered	**sistiméno**
reverse-charge (collect) call	**plirotéo apó to paralípti**
person-to-person (personal) call	**prosopikí klísi**

COMPLAINTS *(parápona)*

Your hotel manager, the proprietor of the establishment in question, or your travel-agency representative should be your first recourse if you have a complaint to make. If you obtain no satisfaction, the tourist police (see POLICE on page 121) will be interested to hear about anything you feel is wrong. All hotels and public places of amusement are price-controlled by the government. If it can be proved that you have been overcharged, the matter will be settled quickly and efficiently.

CRIME (See also EMERGENCIES on page 114 and POLICE on page 121)

Unfortunately, thefts occur more often than they used to, so it's sensible to leave valuables in the hotel safe. Take care of your passport.

Possession of drugs is a serious matter in Greece. Make sure you have a prescription from your doctor if you'll be carrying syringes, insulin, any narcotic drugs, or codeine, which is illegal in Greece.

CUSTOMS and ENTRY FORMALITIES (See also DRIVING on page 112)

Visitors from E.U. countries only need an identity card to enter Greece. Citizens of most other countries must be in possession of a valid passport. European and North American residents are not subject to any health requirements. In case of doubt, check with Greek representatives in your own country before departure.

Duty-free allowance. As Greece is part of the European Union, free exchange of non-duty-free goods for personal use is permitted between Corfu and the U.K. and the Republic of Ireland. However, duty-free items are still subject to restrictions: check before you go. Non-E.U. country residents returning home may bring back the following duty-free amounts: **Australia:** 250 cigarettes **or** 250g tobacco, 1*l* alcohol; **Canada**: 200 cigarettes **and** 50 cigars **and** 400g tobacco; 1.1*l* spirits **or** wine **or** 8.5*l* beer; **New Zealand**: 200 cigarettes **or** 50 cigars **or** 250g tobacco, 4.5*l* wine **or** beer **and** 1.1*l* spirits; **South Africa**: 400 cigarettes **and** 50 cigars **and** 250g tobacco, 2*l* wine **and** 1*l* spirits; **USA**: 200 cigarettes **and** 100 cigars **and** 2kg tobacco, 1*l* wine **or** spirits.

Certain prescription drugs, including tranquillizers and headache preparations, cannot be carried into the country without a prescription or official medical document. Fines—even jail sentences—have been imposed on the unwary tourist.

Currency restrictions. Non-residents may import up to 100,000drs and export up to 10,000drs (in denominations no larger than 5,000drs). There is no limit on the amount of foreign currency or traveller's cheques you may import or export as a tourist, though amounts in excess of $1,000 or its equivalent should be declared to the customs official upon arrival in order to be able to take them out without problems when you leave.

I have nothing to declare.	**Den écho na dilóso típota.**
It's for my personal use.	**Íne giá prosopikí chrísi.**

D

DRIVING

Entering Greece. To bring your car into Greece you'll need:

- A valid driving licence (see below)
- Car registration papers
- Nationality plate or sticker
- Insurance coverage (the Green Card is no longer obligatory within the E.U., but comprehensive coverage is advisable. Contact the Association of Insurance Companies in Athens at 01/323-67330.)

Normally, you may drive a car in Greece for up to four months on your ordinary licence, provided it has been held for one year. An international driving licence (not required for holders of a British licence) is obtainable through your home automobile association.

Driving regulations. The standard European red warning triangle is required in Greece for emergencies. Seat belts are obligatory.

Drive on the right and pass on the left. Greeks have a bad habit of not always returning to the near-side lane, and of passing on the right or left indiscriminately. Traffic from the right has right of way. If a driver flashes lights, it means "Stay where you are," not "Go ahead."

Driving conditions on Corfu. Main roads are generally good, though curves in the road are sometimes indicated too late—or not signposted at all—and they are never banked. Use great care at all times. Secondary roads are sometimes very rough. Drive with extreme caution, as you may be responsible for damages to your rental car. Rock slides are common, particularly in the rainy season. Broken shoulders or holes are not unknown on even the best tarred stretches.

Road signs on main roads and at junctions are in both Greek and Latin letters, but on secondary roads they may be in Greek only.

Gasoline. normal-grade (90-octane), super (98), leadfree, and diesel.

Breakdowns and accidents. For breakdown and accident assistance, contact the Automobile Association of Greece (E.L.P.A.) on tel. **104** (emergencies) or 0661-39504.

Road signs. Most road signs are the standard pictographs used throughout Europe. However, you may also meet these written signs:

ΑΔΙΕΞΟΔΟΣ	No through road
ΑΛΤ/ΣΤΟΜ	Stop
ΑΝΩΜΑΛΙΑ ΟΔΟΣΤΡΩΜΑΤΟΣ	Bad road surface
ΑΠΑΓΟΡΕΥΕΤΑΙ Η ΕΙΣΟΔΟΣ	No entry
ΑΠΑΓΟΡΕΥΕΤΑΙ Η ΣΤΑΘΜΕΥΣΙΣ	No parking
ΔΙΑΒΑΣΙΣ ΠΕΖΩΝ	Pedestrian crossing
ΕΛΑΤΤΩΣΑΤΕ ΤΑΧΥΤΗΤΑ	Reduce speed
ΕΠΙΚΙΝΔΥΝΗ ΝΟΣ ΚΑΤΩΦΕΡΕΙΑ	Dangerous incline
ΕΡΓΑ ΕΠΙ ΤΗΣ ΟΔΟΥ	Roadworks in progress
ΚΙΝΔΥΝΟΣ	Caution
ΜΟΝΟΔΡΟΜΟΣ	One-way traffic
ΠΑΡΑΚΑΜΠΤΗΡΙΟΣ	Diversion (detour)
ΠΟΡΕΙΑ ΥΠΟΧΡΕΩΤΙ ΚΗ ΔΕΞΙΑ	Keep right

Are we on the right road for ...?	**Ímaste stosostó drómo giá ...?**
Full tank, please.	**Na to gemísete me venzíni.**
normal/super/lead-free	**aplí/soúper/amólivdos**
My car has broken down.	**Épatha mía vlávi.**
There's been an accident.	**Égine éna disteíchima.**

E

ELECTRIC CURRENT

Greece has 220-volt, 50-cycle AC current. Sockets are either two- or three-pin. Note that hotels are seldom able to supply plug adapters.

an adapter	**éna metaschimatistí**

EMBASSIES and CONSULATES *(presvía; proxenío)*

Embassies of all major countries are located in Athens. Some countries have consulates in Corfu Town.

British consulate: corner of Alexándras Avenue and Menecrátes Street, Corfu Town (on seafront); tel. 30055 or 37995. Emergency telephone (British embassy, Athens): (01) 723 7727.

Australia: Odos Soútsou 37, 115-21 Athens; tel. (01) 6447-303.

Canada: Gennadíou 4/Ipsilántou, 115-21 Athens; (01) 7239-511.

Ireland: Leofóros Vas. Konstantínou 7, 106-74 Athens; tel. (01) 723-2771. **Consulate** on Corfu, 20a Kapodistríou St; tel. 32469.

New Zealand: Semitélou 9, 115-28 Athens; tel. (01) 7770-686.

South Africa: Leofóros Kifisías 124, 115-26 Athens; (01) 6922-125.

U.K.: Ploutárchou 1/Ipsilántou, 106-75 Athens; tel. (01) 7236-211.

U.S.A.: Leofóros Vas. Sofías 91, 115-21 Athens; tel. (01) 7212-951.

EMERGENCIES (See also MEDICAL CARE on page 117 and POLICE on page 121)

Police (Corfu Town), all-purpose emergency number: **100;** Corfu Town hospital, emergencies: 45811/5 (5 lines); Ambulance service: **166** or **39043;** Fire: **199;** Vehicle emergency: **104.** Note: to call these numbers from outside Corfu Town, you must first dial prefix 0661.

Fire	**Fotiá**
Help	**Voíthia**
Police	**Astinomía**
Stop	**Stamatíste**

G

GUIDES and TOURS *(xenagós; periodía)*

Authorized multi-lingual guide-interpreters work through hotels and travel agencies. Contact the E.O.T. office or the Association of Corfu Travel Agents (see Tourist INFORMATION OFFICES on page 124).

Among the numerous tours offered are those to Paleokastrítsa, the Achílleion, and Corfu Town, as well as Greek nights, boat trips, and day trips to other islands, mainland Greece, and Albania. You can book through travel agents (Auron Expeditions do tours to Albania).

We'd like an English-speaking guide.	**Tha thélame éna xenagó pou milái angliká.**

LANGUAGE

Only in remote countryside spots will non-Greek-speaking tourists have a serious communication problem. Basic English is spoken almost everywhere, as is Italian, German, and French to some degree.

Stress, a very important feature of the Greek language, is indicated in our transcription by an accent mark (´) above the vowel of the syllable to be emphasized.

The table below lists the Greek letters in their capital and small forms, followed by the letters to which they correspond in English.

A	α	a	as in bar
B	β	v	
Γ	γ	g	as in go*
Δ	δ	d	like th in this
E	ε	e	as in get
Z	ζ	z	
H	η	i	like ee in meet
Θ	θ	th	as in thin
I	ι	i	like ee in meet
K	κ	k	
Λ	λ	l	
M	μ	m	
N	ν	n	
Ξ	ξ	x	like ks in thanks
O	o	o	as in got
Π	π	p	

P	ρ	r	
Σ	σ, ς	s	as in kiss
T	τ	t	
Y	υ	i	like **ee** in m**ee**t
Φ	φ	f	
X	χ	ch	as in Scottish lo**ch**
Ψ	ψ	ps	as in ti**ps**y
Ο/ Ω	ω	o	as in g**o**t
ΟΥ	ου	oo	as in s**ou**p

*except before i- and e-sounds, when it's pronounced like y in yes.

You'll find a list of useful expressions on the cover of this guide, and the Berlitz Greek Phrase Book and Dictionary covers practically all the situations you're likely to encounter in your travels.

LOST PROPERTY

Greeks have a reputation for honesty, and Corfu is no exception. If you lose something you have a chance of getting it back. For anything lost away from your hotel, try the tourist police in Corfu Town, tel. 30265, or the security police, 37696. For lost and found at the airport, tel. 33576; for shipping, tel. 39294. Should you lose your passport, report it to the police and contact your consulate in Athens (see page 114). (It's wise to keep a note of your passport details.)

I've lost my
wallet/handbag/passport.

**Échasa to portofóli mou/
ti tsánda mou/to diavatírio
mou.**

MEDIA

Radio and television *(rádio; tileórasi)*. The Greek National Radio (ERT) broadcasts news and weather in English in the morning and afternoon. The English-language newspaper (see below) has times. On shortwave bands, reception of BBC World Service is extremely clear. Voice of America's English programmes are also available.

Television from Athens is available on Corfu, with reception depending on the surrounding terrain. In addition to the three Greek channels, Corfu is also served by two local television channels.

Newspapers and magazines (efimerída; periodikó). During the tourist season foreign-language newspapers are on sale at shops and kiosks on the island. Three English-language monthlies are published on Corfu: *Corfu News* and the *Corfu Sun*, free at the tourist offices, and *The Corfiot*. All have useful information, including bus schedules. The English-language *Athens News* is available.

MEDICAL CARE (See also EMERGENCIES on page 114)

European Union citizens with an E11 form (obtainable in their own country) can have free treatment under the Greek health service. However, it's advisable to take out private holiday medical insurance, as hospital facilities are over-stretched in the tourist season.

Doctors and **dentists** are concentrated in Corfu Town; your hotel will be able to find you one who speaks English. Most resorts have a local surgery, with hours and telephone numbers posted.

The capital's **hospital** and **clinics** operate a 24-hour emergency service which dispatches ambulances (tel. 166 or 39043) to any point on the island with admirable speed. Otherwise, call the all-purpose emergency number **100,** or the tourist police (see POLICE on page 121).

Corfu **General Clinic** is located on the national Paleokastrítsa Road, just outside Corfu Town centre, tel. 0661-36044 or 22946. Corfu **General Hospital** is situated on Policroníou Konstantá Street in Corfu Town, tel. 0661-45811/5 (5 lines); emergencies 166.

Pharmacies (ΦAPMAKEIO—*farmakío*). A red or green cross on a white background identifies a pharmacy (chemist). They are open during normal shop hours (see OPENING HOURS on page 120). One pharmacy is always open in Corfu Town at night and on Saturday and Sunday. Pharmacies display details of night and weekend services.

Without a prescription, you can't get sleeping pills, barbiturates, or medicine for stomach upsets. For import of prescription drugs, see CRIME on page 110 and CUSTOMS AND ENTRY FORMALITIES on page 111.

a doctor/a dentist	**énas giatrós/énas odontogiatrós**
hospital	**nosokomío**
an upset stomach	**varistomachiá**
sunstroke	**ilíasi**
a fever	**piretós**

MONEY MATTERS (See also CUSTOMS and ENTRY FORMALITIES on page 111 and OPENING HOURS ON page 20.

Currency *(nómisma)*. Greece's monetary unit is the drachma *(drachmi*, abbreviated "drs"—in Greek, ΔΡΑΧΜΕΣ).

Coins: 5, 10, 20, 50, 100 drs.
Banknotes: 50, 100, 500, 1,000, 5,000, 10,000 drs.

Banks and currency exchange (ΤΡΑΠΕΖΑ—*trápeza*; ΣΥΝΑΛΛΑΓΜΑ—*sinállagma*). You'll find banks in Corfu Town only, but several bank buses tour the island, and hotels and tourist offices are authorized to change money. You'll need your passport as identification to change money (but not if changing cash).

Credit cards *(pistotikí kárta)*. Internationally known credit cards are honoured in many shops (indicated by a sign in the window) and by banks, car rental firms and leading hotels, but you will generally have to pay an additional 5-7% for the privilege of using them.

A better option is to use the cashpoint machines outside main banks, which accept major cards (instructions in several languages).

Traveller's cheques. Most major brands of traveller's cheques, in any Western currency, are readily cashed. Always take your passport for identification. Eurocheques are now accepted in many places.

I want to change some	**Thélo na alláxo merikés**
pounds/dollars.	**líres/meriká dollária.**
traveller's cheques	**taxidiotikés epitagés**

Can I pay with this credit card?   **Boró na pliróso me aftí ti pistotikí kárta?**

PLANNING YOUR BUDGET

The following are average prices. Due to inflation and the fact that prices rise with each new tourist season, they are only approximate.

Airport transfer. Taxi 1,000-1,200drs (day), 1,500 (night).

Babysitters. 1,500drs per hour.

Bicycle and motorscooter rental. *Bicycles* 1,500-2,500drs per day, 7,000-8,000drs per week. *Motorscooters* 3,500-5,000drs per day, 18,900-20,000drs per week.

Bus fares. Corfu Town to: Sidári 460drs; to Paleokastrítsa 320drs; to Ípsos 220drs; to Kávos 600drs.

Camping (average prices per day). 700-900drs per person, tents 800drs, cars 700-800drs, caravans (trailers) 800-900drs.

Car rental (international company, high season). *Seat Marbella* 12,100drs per day, 50drs per km. *Opel Corsa* 14,400drs per day, 60drs per km. *Open jeep* 16,200drs per day, 80drs per km, *Suzuki jeep* 18,000drs per day, 80drs per km. Add insurance and VAT. Note: Local companies are usually cheaper per day for most models.

Cigarettes. Greek brands 300-450drs per packet of 20; foreign brands 450-500drs.

Entertainment. Bouzoúki music evening including a drink, from 5,000drs; disco (with one drink) from 1,000drs; cinema 1,000drs.

Hotels (double room with breakfast, all taxes included). *De luxe* from 30,000drs. *Class A* from 16,000drs. *Class B* 10-12,000drs. *Class C* 8-9,000drs. *Class D* 6-7,000drs.

Meals and drinks. Continental breakfast 1,500-2,500drs. Lunch or dinner in fairly good establishment 2,000-5,000drs; coffee (instant) 450drs, oúzo with mezédes 450drs, Greek brandy 500drs, gin and tonic 600drs, beer 400drs, wine 400 drs, soft drinks 280drs.

Museums. Adults 400-800drs, children and seniors 200-400drs.

Corfu

Sports. *Sunbeds and beach umbrellas* 300-500drs each. *Yacht* from 15,000drs per day. *Water-skiing* 4,000drs for 10 minutes. *Parasailing* 6,500drs 1 person, 9,500drs 2 persons. *Golf* green fees 5,000-10,000drs per day. *Tennis* from 2,000drs per person per hour.

OPENING HOURS (See also PUBLIC HOLIDAYS on page 122)

Shops. Shops are generally open on Monday, Wednesday and Saturday from 8:30am until 2pm, and on Tuesday, Thursday and Friday from 8:30am until 1:30 or 2pm and again in the evening from 5pm until 8:30 or 9pm. Most shops in Corfu Town shut on Sunday, except those catering for tourists, which often stay open through the siesta. Some larger supermarkets on the outskirts of town are open Monday to Saturday from 8am to 9pm, and Sunday from 9am to 2pm.

Siesta. By 2:30 or 3pm at the latest, Corfu effectively shuts down for its siesta. People riding motorscooters or playing radios loudly in siesta time are liable to a fine for disturbing the peace. If you telephone a Corfiote you risk his or her extreme displeasure. People re-emerge and shops reopen about 5pm, when the worst heat is over.

Museums. Museum hours vary, but museums are generally open Tuesday to Sunday from 8:30 or 9am to 3pm; most are closed on Monday.

Banks. During the high season, the banks are open Monday to Friday from 8am to 1:30 or 2pm.

Post offices. Hours are usually Monday to Friday from 7:30am to 8pm (till 2:30pm for money orders and parcels).

PHOTOGRAPHY and VIDEO

A photo shop is advertised by the sign ΦΩΤΟΓΡΑΦΕΙΟ *(fotografío)*. Major brands of colour and black-and-white film are available, but prices are higher than at home. Polaroid film is difficult to find. The odd shop in Corfu Town sells blank video tapes, but it's safest to bring your own supply.

Some museums charge for photography, particularly if you use a flash. For security reasons, it's illegal to use a telephoto lens aboard an aircraft, nor may you photograph the airport, police stations, or army lookout post over Albania from above Ágios Stéfanos (Siniés).

For handy tips on how to get the most out of your holiday photographs, purchase a copy of the Berlitz-Nikon Pocket Guide to Travel Photography (available in the U.K. only).

I'd like a roll of film	**Tha íthela éna film giaftí ti**
for this camera	**michaní.**
colour slides	**énchromo film giá sláïds**
35mm film	**éna film triánda pénde milimétr**
How long will it take to develop (and print) this film?	**Se póses iméres boríte na emfanísete(ke na ektipósete) aftó to film?**
May I take a picture?	**Boró na páro mía fotografía?**
video tape	**miá vídeo-kasséta**

POLICE (ΑΣΤΥΝΟΜΙΑ—*astinomía*) (See also EMERGENCIES on page 114)

The Security Police and Aliens Police share headquarters, where they deal with major crimes, resident and work permits, and crimes involving visitors. You'll recognize these officers by their uniforms —grey or blue, short- or long-sleeved, depending on the season.

The Tourist Police (*touristikí astinomía*) help visitors personally and also accompany state inspectors to hotels and restaurants to ensure that proper standards and prices are maintained.

If you need to report a loss or theft to the police, go to the police station closest to the scene of the crime. Each group of villages has a police station—you'll have to find out where, and go there.

When on Corfu, E.U. members have the same rights, by law, as any Greek citizen. Your consulate will be able to advise on legal matters.

Corfu

The traffic police check car documents, operate speed traps and issue fines for illegal parking (fines in Greece are high).

Emergency telephone number	**100**
Tourist police	**30265**
Security police	**37696**
Aliens police	**39494**
Traffic police	**39050, 22353**
Where's the nearest police station?	**Pou íne to kodinótero astinomikó tmíma?**

PUBLIC HOLIDAYS *(argíes)*

Banks, offices, and shops are closed on the following national holidays, as well as during some feasts and festivals (see page 90):

1 January	*Protochroniá*	New Year's Day
6 January	*ton Theofaníon*	Epiphany
25 March	*Ikostí Pémti Martíou (tou Evangelismoú)*	Greek Independence Day
1 May	*Protomagiá*	May Day
21 May	*Énosis ton Eptaníson*	Ionian Union Day
15 August	*Dekapendávgoustos (tis Panagías)*	Assumption Day
28 October	*Ikostí Ogdóï Oktovríou*	Òchi ("No") Day, celebrating defiance of Italian ultimatum and invasion of 1940
25 December	*Christoúgenna*	Christmas Day
26 December	*défteri iméra ton Christougénnon*	St. Stephen's Day
Moveable dates:	*Katharí Deftéra*	1st Day of Lent: Clean Monday
	Megáli Paraskeví	Good Friday
	Deftéra tou Páscha	Easter Monday

Análipsis	Ascension
tou Agíou Pnévmatos	Whit Monday
	("Holy Spirit")

Note: The dates on which the moveable holy days are celebrated often differ from those in Catholic and Protestant countries.

RELIGIOUS SERVICES

The national church is the Greek Orthodox. Services start around 8:30am on Sunday and feast days and last about 2½ hours. Visitors of other faiths can attend the following services:

Catholic. The cathedral of St. James on the Town Hall Square holds services daily June-Sept at 8am and Oct-May at 8:30am; also Saturday at 7pm. Sunday services at 8:30am, 10am, and 6pm.

Anglican. Holy Trinity Church at Mavíli 21 has Sunday morning prayer at 9:45, Communion at 10:30, and evening worship at 7pm.

Jewish. The synagogue is on Velissáriou St., near the New Fort.

TIME DIFFERENCES

The chart below shows the time difference between Greece and various cities. In summer, Greek clocks are put forward one hour.

	New York	London	**Athens**	Jo'burg	Sydney	Auckland
winter:	5am	10am	**noon**	noon	9pm	11pm
summer:	5am	10am	**noon**	11am	7pm	9pm

TIPPING

By law, service charges are included in the bill at hotels, restaurants, and tavernas. The Greeks aren't tip-crazy, but expect you to leave a little more if service has been good. Waiters will probably have *a mikró* (an assistant), who should get a token of appreciation as well.

Corfu

Hotel porter	200drs per bag
Hotel maid	500drs per day
Waiter	5-10% (*optional*)
Taxi driver	10% (*optional*)
Tour guide	300drs (*optional*)
Hairdresser/barber	10%
Lavatory attendant	50drs

TOILETS (ΤΟΥΑΛΕΤΤΕΣ—*toaléttes*)

In Corfu Town there are public conveniences on Platia G Theotóki, near the Esplanade bandstand, opposite Barclays Bank in San Rocco Square, and at the square in the Old Port. If there's someone in attendance you should leave a small tip. In cafés, if you drop in specifically to use the facilities, it's customary to have a coffee or some other drink before leaving. Except in modest establishments, there are generally two doors, marked °À¡∞πKø¡ (ladies) and ∞¡¢ƒø¡ (gentlemen).

Note: if there's a waste bin, you're expected to put toilet tissue in that—not down the toilet. Toilets easily become clogged!

Where are the toilets? **Pou íne i toaléttes?**

TOURIST INFORMATION OFFICES (*grafío pliroforión tourismoú*)

The Greek National Tourist Organization staff can provide assistance in preparing for your trip and while you're in Corfu. They supply a wide range of accurate, colourful brochures and maps for the region in various languages, and can generally give information on hotels, campsites and itineraries.

Australia: 51-57 Pitt Street, Sydney, NSW 2000; tel. (02) 241 1663

Canada:1300 Bay Street, Toronto, Ont M5R 3K8; tel. (416) 968 2220; 1233 rue de la Montagne, Montreal, Que. H3G 1Z2; tel. (514) 871 1535

U.K.: 4 Conduit Street, London W1R 0DJ; tel. 0171-734-5997

U.S.A.: 645 Fifth Avenue, New York, NY 10022; tel. (212) 421 5777; 611 W 6th Street, Los Angeles, CA 90017; tel. (213) 626-6696; 168 N Michigan Avenue, Chicago, IL 60601; tel. (312) 782-1084

The main Corfu office of the National Tourist Organization of Greece (*Ellinikós Organismós Tourismoú*, abbreviated E.O.T.), is located at No 1, New Port, Corfu Town; tel. 0661 37520 or 37638/9. It is open Monday to Friday from 8am to 2pm.

In addition to the E.O.T., the municipality of Corfu (tel. 20455/6) operates information kiosks from April to September, with information about events and services in Corfu Town, and also currency-exchange facilities. They are at the Esplanade, San Rocco Square, and Solomou Square; open from 9am until 9pm daily except Sunday.

Another source of information is the Association of Corfu Travel Agents, 33 Spírou Vassilíou St., 49100 Corfu; tel. 0661-21521.

Where's the tourist office?   **Pou íne to grafío tourismoú?**

TRANSPORT

Buses (*leoforío*). The island's public bus service is efficient and good value. Timetables are displayed at bus-stops (ΣΤΑΣΙΣ — *stásis*) in the capital and are also available from the E.O.T. (see TOURIST INFORMATION OFFICES above). There are no all-night bus services.

There are two types of buses. The blue town buses serve towns and villages in the vicinity of Corfu Town and leave from San Rocco Square. Buses for Kanóni depart near the Esplanade. Country buses are green and cream-coloured, and leave from the coach station on I. Theotóki. Tel. 31595 for blue buses, 30627 or 39985 for green buses. You can buy your tickets on the bus or from kiosks in the square.

What's the fare to ...?   **Piá íne i timí giá ...?**

When's the next bus to ...?   **Póte févgi to epómeno leoforío giá ...?**

single (one-way)/   **apló/me epistrofí**
return (round-trip)

Corfu

Taxis (ΤΑΞΙ—*taxí*). Taxis are based in Corfu Town (blue ones) and also in the country (grey). Taxi ranks in town are at the Old Port, Spilia, Esplanade, Pallas Cinema, and San Rocco Square. There are two rates on the meter, a slow one used in Corfu Town and on two-way journeys, the other a fast rate for single out-of-town trips (meter changed from slow to fast rate at town boundary). Radio taxis can be called on 33811/2 or 41333; there's a 200drs surcharge.

Ferries and boats. For current information on ferries to the mainland and other islands, check with the E.O.T. or a travel agent. If you're catching a late-night ferry, there are private companies that handle baggage storage across from the Customs House; they are not open all day, however, and it may be easier to store bags at the hotel.

Small boats can be hired at most resort areas for sightseeing along the coast and day trips to secluded beaches. You should be experienced with boats before taking one out on your own, however.

Horse-cabs (*ámaxa me álogo*). You'll see several dozen of these handsome 19th-century buggies around Corfu Town. They're also known by the Italian name *carrozza*. Be sure to agree on a fare.

What's the fare to ...?   **Piá íne i timí giá ...?**

TRAVELLERS WITH DISABILITIES

Travellers with special needs can contact the Association of Corfu Travel Agents, 33 Spírou Vassilíou Str, 49100 Corfu, tel. 0661-21521, with enquiries about hotels, tours, etc.

TRAVELLING TO CORFU

By Air

International flights: the only direct flights to Corfu are on charter airlines. All scheduled flights to Corfu go via Athens. Olympic Airways operates daily between Athens and Corfu, a 35-minute trip.

From the UK and Ireland: there is a wide selection of package tours and seat-only flights to Corfu, from April to October. Prices vary according to tour operator, time of travel, and the kind of accommodation. Most travel agents recommend cancellation insurance.

From North America: Economical charter flights are arranged by clubs or associations for members and immediate families. Also try your travel agent for tour operators' packages to Corfu. Various airlines offer services to Athens from New York, Boston, and Montreal.

By Rail

The most direct route passes through Paris and Berne to Italy (Brindisi or Ancona), where you catch the ferry to Corfu.

For European residents, Inter-Rail tickets are valid in Greece. Non-European residents can travel on an unlimited-mileage Eurailpass ticket—valid for first-class travel in continental Western Europe.

By Road

Due to the conflicts in the former Republic of Yugoslavia, it is no longer recommended that travellers make the journey from northern Europe to Greece by road. You can, however, drive through France and Italy and catch an Italy-Greece ferry. Advance booking is strongly recommended.

Some coach operators offer trips from London and continental Europe to Athens, where you can catch a flight or a ferry to Corfu.

By Sea

In summer, there is a daily car-ferry service from Brindisi, Italy, leaving at night and arriving in Corfu the following morning. This is also the main route for the rucksack crowd travelling by InterRail, so it can be crowded. Luxury boats leave from Ancona, Italy, and take 24 hours to cross.

The main ferry lines to the Greek mainland link Corfu to Patras and Igoumenítsa (a 2-hour trip). There are also car-ferry services from Bari, Otranto, Venice, and Trieste (though only in high season). Check schedules.

W

WATER *(neró)*

Corfu's tap water is not really considered safe to drink, even in Corfu Town. Bottled mineral water *(metallikó neró)* is readily available.

WEIGHTS and MEASURES

Greece always uses the metric system.

Temperature

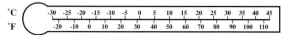

Fluid measures

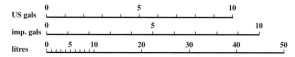

Distance

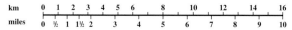

Y

YOUTH HOSTELS (ΞΕΝΩΝ ΝΕΟΤΗΤΟΣ — *xenón neótitos*)

Corfu has one official youth hostel, at Kontokáli, 7 km (4 miles) from Corfu Town, with a total of 30 beds, segregated dormitory style. There's an extra charge if you take a hot shower or have sheets laundered. It's a good idea to inspect the hostel before checking in.

Recommended Hotels

All hotels are classified by the National Tourist Organization (see page 124), but this only establishes minimum rates, and prices can often vary widely within each band according to the season, location, and availability of rooms. Rates must, by law, always be posted in all the rooms.

When booking through a travel agent at home, try to determine the proximity of your hotel to the beach and town. Some hotels are situated up rather steep hills, and may be a good 15 minutes walk or more along a main road to town, which can be difficult for people with physical ailments or young children.

Most hotels get booked up quickly for the high season (from mid-June until October and in particular around the middle of August), so make sure that you reserve well ahead.

All rooms listed here are "C" class or above. Prices quoted are for a double room with bath, but without breakfast, in high season. Most hotels on the island are open for the whole year round, but be sure to call ahead if going off-season.

Finally, note that more modest hotels might not accept credit-card payment, and you may be asked to pay in advance.

✪	Under 10,000drs
✪✪	10,000-20,000drs
✪✪✪	Above 20,000drs

CORFU TOWN

Archontico ✪✪ *Athanassíou 61, Garítsa; Tel. 0661-37222.* This converted mansion is 15-20 minutes walk to the south of the Esplanade along the sea front. In addition to its old-fashioned ambience, the hotel can offer a variety of modern amenities, including a pleasant garden café and bar. Note that there is some traffic noise at the front. 29 rooms.

Arkadion ✪ *Kapodistríou St., Corfu Town; Tel. 0661-37670.* Rooms are somewhat small and there's lots of street noise, but you can't beat the location—right on the Esplanade at the southern end of the Listón! The staff here are friendly, and the hotel offers good value for money. 95 rooms.

Corfu

Atlantis ✪-✪✪ *Xenofóntos Stratigoú St. 48, Corfu Town; Tel. 0661-35560.* Situated on the busy main road across from the Customs House at the New Port, 10 minutes walk from the town centre, this hotel offers clean rooms, free parking, restaurant and bar. 112 rooms.

Bella Venezia ✪✪ *N. Zambéli 4, Corfu Town; Tel. 0661-46500.* This modern, 3-star hotel is in a lovely, renovated historic building, right in the centre, and is popular with locals and visitors. 61 rooms.

Cavalieri ✪✪ *Kapodistríou St. 4, Corfu Town; Tel. 0661-39041.* A 4-star establishment in a lovely old mansion across from the Esplanade, the hotel has its own roof garden. 91 rooms.

Corfu Palace Hotel ✪✪✪ *Leofóros Democratías 2, Corfu Town; Tel. 0661-39485; fax 31749* All rooms have a sea view in this luxury hotel overlooking Garítsa Bay, just south of the Esplanade. Beautiful grounds with subtropical gardens border the old Venetian city walls. The hotel's many amenities include air-conditioning, indoor and outdoor swimming pools, and restaurants. 110 rooms.

NORTHEAST COAST

Hotel Aleka ✪ *Kondokáli; Tel. 0661-91291; fax 91681; or Thompson Simply Greece (London); tel. 0181 200 8733.* In a pretty garden setting on the hillside above Kondokáli Village, 15 minutes walk from the beach and village centre, the hotel offers comfortable rooms, pool, billiards, tennis court, poolside bar, breakfast room, and motorbike rentals.

Chandris Hotels ✪✪✪ *Dassiá Bay; Tel. 0661-97100; fax 93458.* Chandris operates two large hotels—Corfu and Dassiá—on Dassiá Bay, separated from the sea by large private gardens. Rooms are in main buildings, bungalows or chalets. Facilities include air-conditioning, swimming pool, tennis, restaurants, disco. Half board is compulsory in high season. Corfu Chandris offers 301 rooms; Dassiá Chandris has 251 rooms.

Dassiá Beach Hotel ✪✪ *Dassiá; Tel. 0661-93224.* Situated right beside the beach, the rooms here all have balconies, some overlooking the sea. There is a waterfront taverna. 102 rooms.

Kondokáli Bay Hotel ✪✪✪ *Kondokáli; Tel. 0661-38736; fax 91901.* This deluxe hotel 6 km (4 miles) north of Corfu Town boasts beautiful gardens along the sea, pool and private beach, restaurant, taverna, beach bar, and tennis courts. Most rooms have sea or garden views. 152 rooms, 81 bungalows.

NORTH COAST

Acharávi Beach Hotel ✪✪ *Acharávi; Tel. 0663-63146.* A friendly, modern establishment right on the beach, the hotel offers a pool, restaurant, and tennis. 82 rooms and 20 bungalows.

Ionian Princess Hotel ✪✪ *Acharávi; Tel. 0663-63110.* Built in the traditional Greek-villa style, this hotel is 5 minutes walk from the beach and has a restaurant, pool, gardens, tennis, and rooms with balconies. 300 rooms.

Hotel Róda Beach ✪✪ *Róda,. Tel. 0663-63202.* This is a large hotel outside town, with extensive gardens that lead down to the beach, three swimming pools, tennis, restaurants and bar. 393 rooms.

Sellas Hotel ✪-✪✪ *Sidári; Tel. 0663-95500.* A quiet hotel located 10 minutes away from the town centre, and 5 minutes from the Canal d'Amour, it offers spacious rooms with balconies, swimming pool, restaurant and bar. 21 rooms.

Silver Beach Hotel ✪-✪✪ *Róda; Tel. 0663-63112.* Small and relaxed, this family-run hotel is located 3 minutes from the beach, and has a pool, restaurant, bar, and large gardens. 63 rooms.

WEST COAST

Akrotiri Beach Hotel ✪✪ *Paleokastrítsa; Tel. 0663-41237.* This modern establishment stands on a headland overlooking the sea, and offers air-conditioned rooms with verandahs, swimming pool, restaurants, bar, shops. 236 rooms.

Corfu

Ermónes Beach Hotel ✪✪-✪✪ *Ermónes; Tel. 0661-94241.*
Bungalows built on hillside terraces high above Ermónes Bay are
linked by lift to a restaurant and pool above and the beach below.
Tennis and watersports are available, and golf nearby. 272 rooms.

Glyfáda Beach Hotel ✪✪ *Glyfáda; Tel. 0661-94258.* A quiet
hotel set on the beach at the north end of the road, this has large
rooms with balconies facing the sea, and two tavernas nearby.

Grand Hotel Glyfáda Beach ✪✪-✪✪✪ *Glyfáda; Tel. 0661-
94201.* One of the island's best hotels stands at the southern end of
the beach. The furnishings are sumptuous; amenities include a pool,
two restaurants, bar, disco and live music, watersports. 242 rooms.

Paleokastrítsa Hotel ✪✪ *Paleokastrítsa; Tel. 0663-22117.*
Set on a hillside overlooking the beach 10 minutes walk away, this
hotel has two pools, a restaurant, bar, and nightclub. 163 rooms.

SOUTH COAST

Apollo Palace ✪✪-✪✪✪ *Messongí; Tel. 0661-75433.* The
modern hotel complex here, a short walk from the beach, has its
own gardens, pool, tennis, restaurant, and bar. 71 rooms.

Corfu Hilton ✪✪✪ *Nafsikás Street, Kanóni; Tel. 0661-36540.*
This deluxe hotel overlooks a private beach and is close to a viewpoint for Mouse Island. It offers two pools, tennis, bowling alley,
health facilities, garden, restaurants, bars, and casino. 274 rooms.

Delfinakia ✪✪ *Moraítika. Tel. 0661-33045.* This is a complex of two small hotels, 40 rooms each, set in an olive grove
100m from a private beach. It offers rooms with balconies, a
pool, tennis, beach bar, and grill.

Potamaki ✪✪ *Benítses; Tel. 0661-30889.* Facing a shingle
beach, this large hotel is popular with British holidaymakers. Its
rooms have balconies, and there's also a pool, bar, restaurant,
gardens. 150 rooms.

Recommended Restaurants

In Corfu Town you can eat well in modest little tavernas at very reasonable prices, or enjoy a cosmopolitan dining scene at several restaurants serving international cuisine. In the resort areas you'll find a range of restaurants catering for the tourist trade. Restaurants in Corfu Town are open year-round. Reservations are only advisable for top restaurants in high season.

A cover charge of 100-200drs is standard. Service is included in the bill, but it's customary to leave a bit more. The following prices are per person, for a two-course meal together with cover, service, and a half bottle of wine.

✪	under 2,500drs
✪✪	2,500-5,000drs
✪✪✪	Over 5,000drs

CORFU TOWN

Albatros ✪✪✪ *Corfu Palace Hotel, Leofóros Democratías 2; Tel. 39485.* International and local specialities served in this distinguished grill room of the Corfu Palace Hotel. Live music is also provided.

Averof ✪-✪✪ *Prosaléndou St. 4m; Tel. 31468.* Well-known, busy restaurant situated down a narrow street a little inland from the Old Port; there is a wide selection of dishes to be sampled, as well as a variety of Corfiote house wine on offer.

Chrissomállis ✪ *N. Theotóki 6; Tel. 30342* This simple taverna and grill room just off the Listón serves a selection of grilled meats and Greek specialities, including pastitsádo, sofríto, moussaká.

Cofineta ✪✪-✪✪✪ *Kapodistríou 96; Tel. 25642.* Restaurant and bar in a splendid location near the palace at the top of the Listón. Tables are arranged around a lovely bright flower garden. There is an Italian and Continental menu with some Greek dishes also available. Scrumptious selection of ice-cream sundaes.

133

Corfu Pizza ✪ *Kapodistríou 6; Tel. 35976.* The restaurant is located close to the bandstand on the Esplanade. It is reputed to serve the best pizza in town. However, there is also an interesting selection of Greek specialities on offer.

La Cucina ✪ *Gylford Street 15; Tel. 45029.* Cheap and cheerful establishment, serving principally pizza, a variety of pastas, and salad. The restaurant is able and willing to deliver, if you should so desire.

Gallery Inn ✪ *On small side street off Spir, near St. Spyrídon's.* At this small wine bar you can order delicious homemade sandwiches and burgers. It is closed, however, on Saturday evening and throughout Sunday.

Gerékos ✪✪-✪✪✪ *Kondokáli Village. Tel. 91281.* Authentic fish taverna. Whether you dine at the original taverna or its sister restaurant (which goes under the same name) across the road, service is friendly and the fish exquisitely prepared. For a particularly tasty starter, try the boullaibaisse. There is also good house white wine available.

Olympia Café ✪ *Listón 24.* This most French of all the cafés under the arcades still retains its original French décor inside, with marvellous green marble tabletops, mahogony-panelled mirrors, and an array of sculpted wood ceiling decorations.

Oréstes ✪✪✪ *Xen. Stratigoú St. 78; Tel. 35664.* Good seafood restaurant situated near the New Port, together with an outdoor garden. There is also Greek cuisine on offer.

Pántheon ✪ *Prosaléndou St. 16; Tel. 30921.* This restaurant serves traditional Greek cuisine, and is located in a narrow street close to the Old Port.

Port ✪-✪✪ *El. Venizélou St. 36 (Xen. Stratigoú St.); Tel. 30921.* Here you can dine alongside the small-boat harbour. The restaurant offers principally Corfu specialities and fresh local fish.

Restaurant Argó ✪✪✪ *Eth. Antistásseos; Tel. 24398.* This establishment serves excellent fresh fish and seafood. The restaurant is located a short distance from the New Port.

Rex ✪✪ *Kapodistríou St. 66; Tel. 39649.* Busy, well-frequented restaurant which is situated just behind the Listón. It usually serves predominantly Greek cuisine.

Spaghettiano ✪ *Along the port, near Coco Flash disco.* As its name suggests, the restaurant here serves pasta or spaghetti to please everyone's tastes.

Taverna Trípa ✪✪✪ *Kinopiástes (7 km/4 miles southwest of town); Tel. 56333.* This marvellous, award-winning restaurant is a must! Countless celebrities and heads of state have come here, and continue to do so. The authentic old taverna serves superb Greek cuisine. Dining is on a large, vine-covered patio. There is an array of delectable starters, which may be followed by spit-roasted lamb or pheasant, as well as a fine selection of desserts and wine. Greek music and folk dancing takes place. It's wise to book ahead in high season.

Venetian Well Bistro ✪✪✪ *Kremastí Square; Tel. 44761.* Romantic dining around a 17th-century Venetian wellhead, to the subdued strains of classical music. The restaurant's imaginative menu changes every day, featuring such dishes as wild boar, duck in kumquat sauce, or chicken in Champagne. There is a good wine list, and service is attentive. One of the best restaurants in Corfu Town.

Xeníkhtis ✪✪-✪✪✪ *Potamoú St. 12; Tel. 24911.* Situated on the main road north, just out of the town centre, the restaurant offers Greek, French, and Italian cuisine; also steaks. Intimate atmosphere, and live music occasionally. Closed on Sundays.

Yisdhákis ✪ *Solomoú 20; Tel. 37578.* Authentic Greek kitchen, where you won't automatically be served chips! You can choose from a variety of daily specials, all simmering under the glass counter.

ABOUT BERLITZ

In 1878 Professor Maximilian Berlitz had a revolutionary idea about making language learning accessible and enjoyable. One hundred and twenty years later these same principles are still successfully at work.

For language instruction, translation and interpretation services, cross-cultural training, study abroad programs, and an array of publishing products and additional services, visit any one of our more than 350 Berlitz Centers in over 40 countries.

Please consult your local telephone directory for the Berlitz Center nearest you or visit our web site at http://www.berlitz.com.

Helping the World Communicate